PHOTOGRAPHERS' BRITAIN

NORTHUMBERLAND

PHOTOGRAPHERS' BRITAIN

NORTHUMBERLAND

J.C. TORDAI

ALAN SUTTON

First published in the United Kingdom in 1993
Alan Sutton Publishing Ltd · Phoenix Mill · Far Thrupp · Stroud · Gloucestershire

First published in the United States of America in 1993
Alan Sutton Publishing Inc. · 83 Washington Street · Dover · NH 03820

British Library Cataloguing in Publication Data

Tordai, J.C.
Photographer's Britain: Northumberland
I. Title
799.994288

ISBN 0–7509–0100–4

Library of Congress Cataloging in Publication Data applied for

Cover photograph: Carrshield
Title Page photograph: Swinburne
Endpapers: Langley on Tyne

Typeset in 10/11 Sabon.
Typesetting and origination by
Alan Sutton Publishing Limited.
Printed in Great Britain by
The Bath Press, Avon.

ACKNOWLEDGEMENTS

I am indebted to Barney Green, Chris Lewis, Rob Lewis, Sue Lewis, Roberto Marco-tullio, Fiona Merrliss, Dave Panther, Elaine Panther, Jon Rigby, Rhonda Robson and Jackie Williams.

In compiling the notes which accompany the photographs, I have gleaned information from the following recommended studies on Northumberland:

Frank Atkinson, *Life and Tradition in Northumberland and Durham*, J.H. Dent & Sons Ltd, 1977.

David Bean, *Tyneside*, Macmillan, 1971.

Beryl Charlton, *Upper North Tynedale*, Beryl Charlton, 1987.

Tony Hopkins, *Northumberland National Park*, 1987.

Nikolaus Pevsner, *Northumberland*, Penguin, 1974.

T.H. Rowland, *Waters of Tyne*, Abbey Press, 1991.

T.H. Rowland, *Medieval Castles, Towers, Peles and Bastles of Northumberland*, Sandhill Press, 1987.

W.W. Tomlinson, *Comprehensive Guide to Northumberland*, W.H. Robinson, 1889.

Godfrey Watson, *Goodwife Hot*, Oriel Press, 1970.

Geoffrey N. Wright, *The Northumberland Uplands*, David & Charles, 1989.

BLANCHARD

INTRODUCTION

The choice of location and subject for the photographs is intended to reflect some of the county's varied scenery, to include a few of its notable historic buildings and landmarks, and to achieve a reasonable geographic spread of the chosen sites. A few of the photographs reflect scenes which, within a few years, will have disappeared altogether or have been transformed beyond easy recognition. Such scenes belong to that part of the landscape, often, but not exclusively, the urban and the industrial, which undergoes a continual evolution. Other photographs recall the passage of a few memorable events of the twentieth century which, as it draws to a close, somehow mark the end of an era. A few photographs mimic scenes which have been recorded several times by others reaching as far back as the turn of the nineteenth century or earlier. Beyond this though, the photographs reflect personal choices, a favourite haunt or some other association with the place in question over the years.

The accompanying text provides a brief historical sketch or background commentary to the sites or surroundings of the photographs. For those who wish to read more about the county, a number of studies are cited in the text, notable among them the works by Tony Hopkins, T.H. Rowland and Geoffrey N. Wright.

BERWICK-UPON-TWEED

Few towns in Britain can have had as turbulent a history as Berwick. Lying on the River Tweed which demarcates the frontier between England and Scotland, it was fought over incessantly on both sides of the border for nearly three hundred years from the twelfth to the fifteenth centuries. It changed hands thirteen times in this period before finally joining England in 1482. Its history literally shaped the town which, apart from being walled, had at the height of the troubles, nineteen towers along its length and stood at a height of 6.7 metres. In 1558, Elizabeth I had a new wall built, using the expertise of Italian engineers drafted in for the job, specifically to make full use of artillery and to provide fire-cover for all parts of the wall from five bastions. The original wall, which followed the line of the river, was later rebuilt in 1760.

Of the castle, which dates from around 1150, hardly anything now remains. Apart from falling into ruin it stood on the proposed site of the railway station, on what is now the principal route through Northumberland. The railway comes in over Robert Stephenson's Royal Border bridge built in 1850, an impressive structure with 28 arches rising 38 metres above the water. It was Stephenson who also built the High Level bridge, the first rail crossing over the Tyne, and both are superb examples of his talented engineering.

WOOLER

The quaint old petrol pumps of Morton's garage on the outskirts of the town suggest a sleepy rural shire where the steady passage of the seasons beats to an unchanging rhythm. If this is true now, it certainly wasn't in the early parts of its history when Wooler lay at the heart of Northumberland's battlefields, like those of Piperden, Homildon Hill, Hedgeley Moor, Millfield and Geteringe. Most decisive of all was the battle of nearby Flodden Field where James IV of Scotland engaged the English Army in 1513. This was the last and most bloody conflict between the two nations arising out of their respective grievances, but James had the additional motive of seeking to force Henry VIII to abandon his war against Louis XII in Flanders. The Scots were routed at Flodden Field, losing up to nine thousand men, including James himself, leading members of the nobility, the gentry and even clergy.

For centuries, Wooler has served as the market town of Glendale, several rivers swirl around its hinterland and two of them, Wooler Water and the River Till, meet in the town. Wooler as the head of the barony of Muschamp had a castle in Norman times; the early wooden fortress was replaced by a strong tower built by Sir Thomas Grey of Chillingham in the fifteenth century, though this fell into ruin long ago. While the town needed such protection in the lawless and feuding period when it was a frontier town, its worst ravages came much later as a result of two disastrous fires, one in 1772 and the other in 1862.

BLYTH

There is a narrow spit of land which maroons north Blyth from the rest of the town. On one side there is the sea, on the other the River Blyth. The road has to run 8 kilometres via Cambois before it can rejoin the main part of town, though where the small ferry crosses only 32 metres of water separate the two places. It is a landscape rich in the remains of erstwhile industry, principally connected with coal. In Blyth as with many other towns along the coast, such as Amble or Newcastle, large coal staithes were built in timber along the quaysides in the nineteeth century. Generally, these had chutes which took the coal from the trucks on the wagonway directly into the moored collier below. The coal staithes were also connected to the railway where a locomotive would wait to take away empty trucks or bring in loaded ones. The staithes were designed so that loaded trucks could run along the wagonway under gravity, as far along as the chute, and once emptied would return by gravity along a slightly lower track. There is some suggestion that Blyth had an inclined railway in the seventeenth century, before the introduction of the staithes, when the wagonway led down to the harbour itself. The empty trucks then had to be pushed back up but the incline was gentle.

NINEBANKS

Ninebanks, or nine hills, is a tiny village which sits above the River West Allen. This scene is taken from one of them, and the roofs of the village can faintly be seen at the end of the steep track descending into the valley below. It is a pleasant spot overlooking the mass of Whitfield Fell, which along with the surrounding fells, often has to face severe winters, at times bad enough to isolate the area from its nearest towns. Ninebanks has a tower which probably dates from the fourteenth century and is said to have belonged to Sir John Eden. Above one of its windows is a coat of arms but this is now so eroded as to be undecipherable and any light it may have shed on its history is lost. At the top of its four storeys are two spouts carved in projecting stone, which were apparently destined for pouring molten lead upon assailants. A Jacobean newel staircase was built at the same time as the fourth storey as an addition to the earlier more rudimentary tower.

The church of St Mark was rebuilt in the early English style in 1871. Many of the numerous churches and chapels in the Allendales, lacking in congregations and in clerics, have been converted to better use as homes. There were numerous Christian sects in these parts, and among them were the Quakers, as always doing good works and bringing peace. Ninebanks as well as the surrounding valleys and fells is thinly populated. Some homes are only used at weekends or in the summer; the winters can be prolonged and bleak, adding to the sense of remoteness which this wild landscape inspires.

LANGLEY CASTLE

'While I gaze on it, even at great distance, [it] seems to bid a stern defiance to the attacks of time' wrote J. Hodgson in his *History of Northumberland* about Langley. It was built around 1350 by Thomas de Lucy, possibly on the site of the older home of the Tindals, to protect his property from marauding Scots. It passed into the hands of the Umfravilles, the Percys, the Nevilles and the Radcliffes. Acquired by the Percys by marriage to the Lucys, it was damaged in the rebellion of 1405 and its interior burnt, and in a 1541 survey it was described as ruinous. To Sir Francis Radcliffe, who purchased it in 1632, the barony gave the title of Viscount and Baron Langley. After the ill-fated uprising of 1715, however, it was forfeited to the Crown along with the rest of Derwentwater properties. By 1749, Langley had been passed to the Governors of Greenwich Hospital and in 1882 was purchased from the Admiralty by Cadwallader Bates who restored it.

What makes Langley interesting is that because it was in ruins for centuries, it never evolved architecturally as did most other castles in the area. It has the manner of an English fortified house and as Tomlinson points out, in his *Comprehensive Guide to Northumberland* (1889), 'Had it continued to be inhabited, it would be sure to have been subjected to all sorts of Perpendicular, Tudor, Elizabethan, Jacobean, Queen Anne, Georgian and Strawberry-hill Gothic alterations and accretions at the cost of architectural purity.'

JESMOND

Vevgeny Zamyatin is chiefly remembered for his dystopian novel *We*. Written in 1920, it churns out a dour and grim vision of a rationalist state set somewhere in the future and was to heavily influence Orwell's *1984*. Zamyatin abhorred inertia and dogma and believed in the idea of a perpetual revolution. Such thoughts were already swilling around his mind when, as a young naval engineer he was posted to Britain to supervise the construction of ice-breakers for the Russian fleet. Part of his visit was spent in Newcastle where the ordered banality of middle-class English life, as he found it in Jesmond, inspired him to write a story, in 1917, not long before he was to return to Russia in time for the October Revolution. The story, 'Islanders', sowed the seeds which were later to germinate in *We*. 'Islanders' was the story of an entropied society, well-regulated but inert:

> By Sunday the stone steps of the houses in Jesmond had as usual been scrubbed to a dazzling whiteness. The houses were old and smoke blackened but the steps shone in white rows, like the Sunday gentlemen's false teeth. The Sunday gentlemen were of course manufactured at a factory in Jesmond, and on a Sunday morning thousands of copies appeared on the streets.

If Zamyatin could return to Jesmond today he would probably find that not so much has changed; many of the same streets are still there and life is as well ordered and regulated as it ever was. Zamyatin, however, returned to Russia where he was later vilified for publishing novels abroad which were considered ideologically unsound. Of this nothing was known in Jesmond.

CHOLLERFORD

Passing close to the North Tyne river this was the track of the Border Counties railway which once ran from Hexham to Bellingham and then on to Hawick across the border. The line, opened in 1862, was 67.5 kilometres long and was built largely in response to the coal and iron workings around Bellingham. This new industry was not to last long and was already failing by the time the railway arrived in Bellingham, rendering the investment in the railway over-ambitious. Even so, the line beyond Bellingham survived until 1958 while the Hexham stretch lasted five years longer. At one time Northumberland could boast an ample and often very scenic rail network but the dichotomy between market forces and social policy proved insurmountable and one after another of the county's railways was forced into closure. At Chollerford, the trains would pass under the rather fine bridge with its five lofty arches, which was built in 1775 only four years after the Great Flood in which almost all of the bridges across the river were destroyed.

Within easy reach of this bridge, away to the west are the remains of two Roman bridges, the first built by Agricola and the second by Hadrian linking the Roman fort of Cilurnum with the east bank of the Tyne. In its day Cilurnum was the largest fort in Northumberland, covering a site of almost 2.5 hectares, and it housed a cavalry regiment of 500 men. It was a part of the Wall's defences and served as a regional headquarters, and its importance was clear to the barbarians who, from the evidence of excavations, burnt the fort three times.

HEXHAM

The Egger Plant, which manufactures chipboard, is Hexham's most distinctive landmark as well as being its largest. Trailing plumes from its stacks act as a beacon whose signals come into view long before anything else. The same thing is true at night when the billowing smoke swirls around the numerous lights and makes them twinkle from a distance. Like other examples of industrial architecture in the region, the plant seems to swing between a raw ugliness and an ethereal beauty, like a moody *jolie laide*. Measured against Hexham's other glories, the Abbey or the Moot Hall, the lifespan of the Egger Plant will be very brief and yet its presence here arouses passions. Many who live in the surrounding valley complain that the plant spoils the pleasing setting and some are convinced it pollutes. Such allegations were lent weight recently when the company was fined for discharging into the River Tyne which runs alongside the plant. It is, though, the town's largest employer and its location has a certain logic to it. The plant is near to a wood supply at Kielder Forest, Hexham is at the geographic centre of Britain with major road links and the town provides the labour.

Few industrial plants in Northumberland can claim such pleasant surroundings as those enjoyed by Egger; there is the majestic cruise of the Tyne, its banks lined with stately beeches and the neat acres moulded by generations of farming which maroon the plant with their greenery. In turn this farmland is flanked by belts of mature woodland on either side of the valley, but even at this distance the Egger Plant smokes defiantly in the fields below.

RIVER NORTH TYNE

The River North Tyne begins its 69 kilometre journey in Deadwater above Kielder and drops through Falstone, Bellingham, Wark, Chipchase, Haughton, Chollerford and on to Warden where it joins the South Tyne. Its flow is controlled by the Kielder dam and, unlike the Allen, its progress is measured and its pace sedate. In the days when fishing was part of a livelihood, a supplementary activity, rather than a sport, the North Tyne was fished by nets or, when these couldn't be used, with trows. The trow appeared as if two halves of a boat had been stuck together, merged in the bow but divided by the stern. It was flat-bottomed with a draught of 30 centimetres and a beam of 35 centimetres. It was about 3 metres in length and extremely slight, but strengthened internally by transverse wedges. Two men would operate the trow: one towards the stern, who guided it with a bang, a long pole; the other who would spear the fish with a leister. The trows would operate in tandem, the leister men with a foot in each trow, looking down into the water below ready to spear their quarry. Trows would be pushed out on the river when the salmon first came up, in order to accustom the fish to the presence of boats. In Tynedale, trows were also used at night by poachers.

COANWOOD

A characteristic of Northumberland's countryside is the practice of stringing up dead moles along fences, made all the easier since the introduction of wire fencing. The mole-catcher leaves his quarry on view so that the farmer can admire his tally and reassure himself that he is getting value for money. The moles are killed because the farmers consider them a nuisance on their land, although at one time they were killed for their fine coats, once widely used for all sorts of things. In due course, it seems inevitable that the practice will die out, as it has in most other parts of the country, but Northumbrians are strong on tradition and changes are slower to arrive here than they seem to be elsewhere in matters of countryside management.

The coal used in the Cupola smelt mills at Whitfield, which operated from 1706 to 1816, came from Coanwood, from the wood where Collan, the provost of Hexhamshire, once lived. Nearby to Coanwood, the Haltwhistle–Alston railway passed, and of the rural branches, it was the first to open, in 1856, and the last to close, in 1976. This line boasted some superb engineering, including the Lambley viaduct which spans the valley between Coanwood and Lambley. The nine-arched viaduct rose to a height of 33.5 metres as it straddled the River South Tyne.

COLLIERSDEAN

For a few years these great lumbering machines will plough back and forth dragging the land for coal. There isn't a miner in sight; Colliersdean is a civil engineering project which only requires a handful of men to run it. Drive past the site and virtually nothing can be seen of it – a neat white fence, a cluster of portacabins and a few parked cars are all there is to be glimpsed. All else is screened by a grass bank adorned with a few red notices warning of danger. One other sign displayed on the fence reads: 'Colliersdean Opencast is expected to produce one million tonnes of premium quality coal – the land will be restored as farmland, commercial and recreational woodland in line with current agricultural needs being an asset to be enjoyed by the local people.'

A discreet and apparently environmentally-conscious operation which, briefly, will scar the landscape and then disappear, seems a very long way from the days when coal was king. Yet only twenty years ago, in 1972 and then again in 1974, who could have doubted the power of the industry. The second strike brought such grave consequences that the Government called an election to ask 'Who rules?'. The industry's beginnings here though had been innocuous enough; a little was mined by the Romans to keep the troops from freezing along the Wall and a little used to feed the sacred flame burning in the temple of Minerva in Bath. Its perhaps most ignominious function, though, had been to provide ballast for the empty grain ships leaving Tyneside for the fens.

LANGLEY ON TYNE

In a triangle formed by the River Allen, the River South Tyne and the bubbling Langley burn, a low fertile ridge somewhat exposed to the northern winds and scattered with a clutch of farmsteads, makes up Langley on Tyne. The ridge has a patchwork of fields enclosed by drystone walls and enlivened by copses and woods. Some of its rich soil is still tilled in the manner of earlier times, though the sight of horses working the land is rare these days. Farmers certainly used horses for power here in the nineteenth century, but as late as 1807 a farmer near Wooler, working in partnership with his brother, wrote that they had 150 oxen in the draught. Less versatile than horses, and slower, oxen were easier to feed, to shoe and to harness. On retirement horses were sold to dog kennels but there was better value in oxen; at the end of their working life, the lean ones would be sold off while the others were fattened for the shambles. Even so, the horse had been in use in the county for centuries and, until the building of turnpike roads in the eighteenth century, it was the only means of conveying freight. The pack-horse, plodding in long convoys, was the only means of carrying loads over great distances and across difficult terrain; and these small, sturdy animals must once have been a familiar sight on the skyline of Northumberland. There was another, and final fling for horse-power on farms when, in 1788, Andrew Meikle first introduced the horse-gin, a mechanical threshing-machine. Its use quickly spread from Scotland into Northumberland and lingered a while until new technology drove the working horse off the landscape.

LANGLEEFORD

This austere farm sits at the head of the Harthope valley within the lee of the Cheviot, Northumberland's highest hill, which belongs in the National Park. From the evidence of deserted villages and field systems, it would seem that the population in these hills was greater in the thirteenth century than it has been before or since. Around the numerous villages, arable land was cultivated in an open-field arrangement involving the breaking up of two or three large fields into a series of narrow strips, or riggs, which were always ploughed in a clockwise direction with the soil slightly banked on one side to create an effect of a ridge and a trough. This allowed water to drain down the troughs and eventually off the cultivated areas. The villagers worked as a community and shared the ox team. The system worked well and gradually more land came under the plough and there are within the Park, as Tony Hopkins observes in his excellent guide, *Northumberland National Park* (1987), entire hillsides which exhibit the characteristic of corrugation as a result of this medieval farming. The sheep and cattle were pushed even further from the expanding village and gradually a plan developed of grazing the herds and flocks way off in the hills for as much time as possible. The shepherds went with them, staying all summer in small huts known as shielings and returning in the autumn to feed the cattle on the stubble and later the hay. This style of farming persisted in these parts as late as Elizabethan times, but gradually fell into decline as the population increased and community practices were no longer workable. Fathers divided their holdings equally among their sons, and each generation had less to live on.

SWINBURNE ESTATE

Swinburne Castle was built after Roger de Widdrington was given permission by Edward III to fortify his mansion at West Swinburne in 1346. At that time Widdrington was High Sheriff and warden of the Middle Marches. By the time of the 1541 Survey it had fallen into ruin though it is unclear why this happened. In any event it was at some point restored because, as T.H. Rowland notes in *Waters of Tyne* (1991), 'in 1596 Sir Robert Kerr of Cessford attacked it and rescued a prisoner'. Of the original castle nothing more remains since it was pulled down by Thomas Riddell who replaced it with a manor house in the early part of the seventeenth century. Thomas Riddell had married the Widdrington heiress and was responsible for beginning the plantations and clearing the lands to make the park. A century later the main house was built, more or less added on to the manor, just to the south of the village of Great Swinburne.

To the west is the Swine Burn, from which the Swinburne family took their name. The burn passes the village and lower down beyond the Hermitage it joins the Coal Burn and together they flow on to Barrasford where they empty into the North Tyne near to the old mill. The well-established park has an impressive standing stone in a broad meadow on its southern boundary; it stands 3.6 metres high, 1 metre broad and 75 centimetres thick and fans out towards the top. Of red stone with vertical grooves and with a few cup marks, it is placed near to three burial barrows in which a Bronze Age jet necklace was discovered. Nearby, too, are primitive cultivation terraces which would have sustained the modest growing of cereals. A little way to the west of this site is White Cottage, shown here, quietly mouldering in a corner of a field and probably used by estate workers or by a gamekeeper. Its unhindered decay has a charm heightened by its fragility, as if at any moment it might suddenly collapse into a heap of rubble.

SEAHOUSES

In the early years of the nineteenth century, the little fishing village of North Sunderland expanded with the building of a new harbour. The work was financed by Lord Crewe, who was keen to export the products of a developing lime-burning industry. The coal needed for this industry came from shallow mines at the east end of the village, an area which grew into what became known as Seahouses. It had a busy port which exported corn in small sailing boats and when, eventually, the lime quarries closed, it was able to adapt to serve the fishing industry. Railways came to the harbour to carry off herring in the form of smoked kippers, a process which some think originated here.

At the turn of the century Seahouses was at its most active: steamers took advantage of the new piers, both nearly 275 metres in length, to bring in salt and take away barrels of salted herring to northern Europe. There were drifters, too, which called in with their black hulls and dark sails, some from Cornwall and others from the Hebrides and Shetland. The port, around which the grey terraces cluster, is still animated with fishing and the pleasure boats which put out for the Farne Islands where St Aidan went in 635 in search of solitude.

CHOLLERTON

The people of Northumberland and of the Scottish Lowlands are pretty much from the same stock. In the bad old days of the Border struggles this fact was overlooked, even forgotten, in the bitter passion of conflict. The Celts were eventually driven back by the Angles so effectively that by the time Edwin became king of a united Northumbria, his northern boundary lay along a line joining the firths of Forth and Clyde. Edwin founded Edinburgh and to the north were the Picts, but to the south the tribes spoke the same language, and linguistic differences were confined mostly to those of inflection and idiom. In this, the boundary was not the Tweed but lay further south, according to *Goodwife Hot* (1986) by Godfrey Watson, and it was politics and not geography which created two peoples. Chillingham, for example, known in the thirteenth century as Chevelingham, is spoken with a hard 'g', like Coldingham across the border in Scotland. Everywhere else in Northumberland to the south of Chillingham, places like Bellingham or Edlingham, are pronounced with a soft 'g' to produce Bellinjum or Edlinjum. For a while, the whole of the North Tyne, as far south as Chollerton, was the private estate of Scottish kings. Chollerton itself was a manor in the barony of Prudhoe and held by the Swinburnes. In 1263, William de Swynburne was treasurer to Queen Margaret, and was paying rent to the Scottish crown.

Chollerton itself is no more than a small hamlet along the eighteenth-century corn road. The small Norman church of St Giles is on the site of an earlier Saxon church. Its pillars, which support the arches in the south aisle are Roman columns taken from their fort at Chesters, while one of the Roman altars is now used as the font. Not far from the village the North Tyne sweeps past, its banks abundant with trees, and flanked with meadows which burst into flower in June.

HARESHAW BURN

At Bellingham, the Hareshaw burn merges with the North Tyne and along the last stretch of its journey it tumbles down a steep, winding dene from Hareshaw Linn, a waterfall which cascades 10 metres to join the dene in a narrow and rocky ravine. Administered by the National Park, the dene is a designated Site of Special Scientific Interest and is equally a place of quiet charm. In the nineteenth century the tenor of daily life in this district was to change considerably when landowners looked beyond agriculture to other ventures from which they could derive an income from the land. The Duke of Northumberland, who owned Hareshaw Common, persuaded no doubt by similar ventures elsewhere in the county, paved the way for the extraction of iron ore on the north bank of the Tyne. The iron field stretched between Bellingham and Greenhaugh and in 1838 ironworks were built and then leased to Baston, Campion and Co. The works comprised two blast furnaces followed by a third two years later, and these were powered by a 120 hp steam-engine and a 70 hp waterwheel. In addition to this, wagonways were laid between the ironworks and nearby Hareshaw Collieries which delivered and extracted coal to fuel the seventy coke ovens on the site. The one drawback, and it was a major one, as Beryl Charlton observes in her intimate portrait *Upper North Tynedale* (1987), was that 'the ironworks had little chance of success; they were so remote that supplies of metal were not only irregular but costly, to produce and to market'. It wasn't long before the ironworks were running at a loss and despite perseverance, by 1848 were forced into closure. More surprising was the attempt to revive the venture in 1855, but this was soon abandoned.

Running to the east of the Hareshaw burn, and for a brief stretch parallel to it, is the Pennine Way. Along this track the faint traces of the erstwhile coal workings can still be seen, evidence that at one time the landscape must have been deeply scarred by this venture. After its brief flirtation with industry, Bellingham once again reverted to what it had always been, a small market town on the edge of wild and uncompromising country.

WALLSEND

The site of the Roman fort of Segedunum overlooks the shipyards of Swan Hunter. The Romans began the Wall here, right down to the banks of the River Tyne, at a place where they knew it to be unfordable, deep enough in fact to launch ships.

From modest beginnings in the middle years of the nineteenth century and through the symbiosis of partnerships, mergers and acquisitions, Swan Hunter has played a leading role in British maritime history. By 1892 the company was manufacturing its own marine engines and boilers for the ships it was building, ushering in what was to be a golden age of ship-building. The first yard, which occupied a 1.6-hectare site with a river frontage of 90 metres, had by 1903 expanded to fill a site of 32 hectares with a river frontage of 1,220 metres. In 1906 the *Mauretania*, built for Cunard, was launched, followed by its sister ship, the *Lusitania*. They were the pride of the Tyne and won back the Atlantic Blue Riband from the Germans and held on to it for twenty-two years. The *Lusitania*, which was also built for Cunard, was sunk by a German U-Boat in 1915. The yards have been the birthplace of over 2,700 ships, including 400 warships, and among an impressive list was the *Ark Royal* in 1981.

STEEL RIGG

Steel Rigg is not much more than a gap in the Whin Sill, along which runs the Roman Wall. The stretch of Wall which runs east of here to Housesteads fort is rather dramatic in its march, and is briefly joined by the Pennine Way before it makes its journey northwards. Hadrian's successor, Antoninus Pius, moved the frontier further north and ordered the building of a new wall, this time of turf, to span the isthmus of the Forth–Clyde. Effective defence of this structure required heavy manning and the venture was too costly to maintain so the Antonine Wall was abandoned. During the occupation, forts both to the north and the south of Hadrian's Wall came under attack, and the Wall itself was breached on several occasions. Ultimately Severus ordered a rebuilding programme between 198 and 208 and, when this was completed, a punitive raid was made against the Caledonians in 209 and 210, but the emperor died before the task was completed. His sons saw no percentage in continuing the campaign and negotiated a peace treaty with the Caledonians. The following century saw peace in the region, and while the rest of the empire was in turmoil, the Wall and its hinterland became a peaceful backwater. By the end of the third century, trouble had again broken out, again because of attempts by British governors to jockey for position in Rome, leaving the northern frontier vulnerable to attack. The emperor Constantius Chlorus, like Severus before him, had the Wall's defences repaired, and came over to Britain to quell unrest. For a while this worked, but continuing strife early in the fourth century culminated in the Barbarian Conspiracy of 367, in which Picts, Scots, Saxons, Franks and Atocotti joined forces to completely rout the Romans, and once more anarchy reigned.

ALLENDALE

On New Year's Eve, the people of Allendale and many from elsewhere in the locality, gather to celebrate the passing of the old year and the arrival of the new one. A throng of revellers spills out from the town's many pubs and inns towards midnight to watch a procession of oddly-garbed locals wander round the square carrying flaming tubs on their heads. After meandering around for ten minutes they then proceed to light a large bonfire in the middle of the square as the clock strikes midnight. As the bonfire blazes, a band strikes up. Midnight is also the signal for first footing, the origin of this ceremony supposedly pagan but more likely a notion of what a pagan ceremony was, developed when lead-mining was in its heyday.

In his *Comprehensive Guide to Northumberland*, written in 1889, W.W. Tomlinson described Allendale as a 'straggling, dreary-looking place' set in a district which is 'bleak and unpicturesque'. Perhaps when Tomlinson visited the town it would have looked in terminal decline, the great lead-mining centre which was no more, or perhaps it was the weather, for the town sits at 426 metres and gets its fair share of Northumberland's uncompromising winds and rain. A sundial on the church of St Cuthbert indicates a latitude of 54' 60" which puts Allendale midway between Cape Wrath and Beachy Head. Surrounding the church are many inns and pubs, far more than would be usual for what is not much above a village in size, but these catered for the miners during the great age of lead-mining in the eighteenth century and during the first half of the nineteenth. At this time there were about twenty mines on the West Allen and fifteen on the East. Mining demanded an abundance of water which the area has in plenty. Everywhere dams were constructed to form reservoirs, which in turn provided the power to drive the machines which crushed the ore or to work the bellows in the furnaces. Armstrong, the pioneer of hydraulic engines, supplied the nine which were in use in the Allendales to aid the mining process. Smelting was another busy activity around the town, and from the mills led long arched horizontal flues which carried the gases to terminal stacks on the moors. Vaporized lead was then recovered from the roof of the flue arches along which the gases travelled.

BAMBURGH

Above a sandy bay an outcrop of rock rises 45 metres, dominating the country all around. The upward sweep of the rock seems to merge with the walls and battlements of Bamburgh Castle, reputedly one of England's finest. The castle extends over 3.2 hectares and dwarfs the small village beneath its walls. The site was first fortified by the early kings of Northumbria and became its capital under King Oswald. The defences later proved rather inadequate when the Danes pillaged it.

Nowadays, the oldest surviving feature of this period is the well sunk to a labour-intensive depth of 45 metres, half of which was through solid basalt. The twelfth-century keep retains its original walls, not unsurprisingly because they are 3–4 metres thick, but much of the castle was prettified for the first Lord Armstrong in the late nineteenth century.

Bamburgh village is not much more than a row of eighteenth-century cottages spaced around a small green. To one side is a church dedicated to Saint Aidan, who died here, and there is also a memorial to Grace Darling, the daughter of the Farne Islands' lighthouse-keeper, who during a violent storm in 1838, rowed out in a coble with her father to help the stricken steamer *Forfarshire*, and rescued nine men. The scene was immortalized in a dramatic painting by Staniland.

BYKER

Byker is a suburb on the eastern edge of Newcastle. It's the sort of place which for no good reason is never mentioned in guidebooks, perhaps because its history has no significance beyond the locality. In many ways, though, it embodies the character of Tyneside. It is set apart from the rest of town by the valley of the Ouse burn and is linked with it by three bridges which span the valley. The latest bridge is on stilts, rather than arches, and carries the Metro across. This carves up Byker more than is seemly, but on the other hand the Metro is a real asset on Tyneside.

Byker anyway has had to endure bold architectural strokes on its landscape. The arc of the Metro bridge echoes that of the Byker Wall behind it. This was an ambitious housing project which broke the mould of high-rise flats but shared their density. There were those who were puzzled by the emphasis on community in this new architecture when, as far as they were concerned, the back-to-back terraces which the Wall replaced, already had a sense of community. But this isn't Byker's only interesting building; under the bridges is the former warehouse of Cluny whisky, imposing and solid. It sits right on the burn and is next to the city farm where small animals appear to the delight of children. Here and there along the Chillingham road are other eye-catching landmarks like the Beavans store or this Magritte-like vista which adorns the face of the old cinema. 'Letuspray' reads the number plate, and what could be more uplifting?

MOHOPE HEAD

This quiet valley is tucked in beneath a triangle of moors, those of Mohope, Coalcleugh and Middle Fell. It is flanked on one side by the West Allen river, and the narrow road climbs up to Mohope Head where it runs out on to the fells. There is a scattering of isolated farmsteads in this gentle, enclosed valley whose verdant pastures are thrown into sharp relief by the surrounding bleak heights. Furness House is an old fourteenth-century bastle which provided shelter and protection to the smallholders and animals alike; in a period of lawlessness even the humble farmstead needed some fortification. In 1510 Mohope Head was known as Upper Mollup which, as Godfrey Watson explains in *Goodwife Hot* (1986), is the place at the head of the valley which was farmed by Mul. From his name, Mul was probably a half-breed, though of what particular hybrid history does not record. In Northumberland, a Hope indicated a strip of land in a valley which was rather sheltered and less liable to flooding than a Haugh, and usually with more fertile soil than was available further up the hill. All of which applies to Mohope.

NEWCASTLE

Seen from the town moor, this western part of Newcastle has a far more agreeable outward allure than when Pennant wrote of the city in 1769. He described Newcastle as 'a large, disagreeable and dirty town. The lower parts are inhabited by keel men and their families, a mutinous race, for which reason the town is always garrisoned'. Had he explored a little further he could have witnessed another, nobler, side to the town's character. In 1775 a precursor to the Literary and Philosophical Society, the Philosophical Society, debated the burning issues of the day. One such debate took place between Thomas Bewick, the genius of wood engraving, and Thomas Spence, the long forgotten author, of the bizarre idea of dividing the produce of the nation equally among all classes of society. These two, engaged in some imponderable discussion from which no resolution seemed possible, decided on an alternative method of settling the question. In *Rambles in Northumberland* (1832), Stephen Oliver recalls that it was resolved 'in the manner in which all knotty points ought to be settled; namely, by the argumentum baculinum – a bout at single-stick'. The floor of the Society's room was the venue for this adventurous style of philosophical debate in which 'the athletic artist had by far the best argument, and proved himself a most powerful reasoner at club logic; and after half an hour's animated discussion, fairly non-plus'd his opponent, and compelled him to acknowledge himself defeated'. It wasn't just the sights and the habits of Newcastle which dismayed those visiting from the south, it was the language as well. Nobody seemed able to understand what people said and this was a centuries-old problem. One early amateur philologian wrote, 'All the language of the Northumbers is to scharp, slitting, and frotynge and unschape, that we southerne men may that longage unnethe understonde,' which puts it in a nutshell.

ASHINGTON

A few centuries ago Ashington would not have rated inclusion on a map and it was no more than its name implied, the Valley of Ash trees. The town owes its existence to coal but the industry around the place is only a pale echo of what it was. The town was built with geometric neatness, laid out in serried ranks of terraced streets and dour estates. Beyond them the hinterland was once dotted with pit-heads and slag heaps, and burning coal smoked in every chimney. Much of this landscape has been remodelled with features such as the riverside walks on the banks of the Wansbeck, the river which flows to the south of the town out past North Seaton Colliery and then empties into the North Sea, or the country park which was built around a lake which profited from a depression caused by mining subsidence. Included in the country park is Woodhorn Colliery, its derelict pit-head gear shown here. Located on the north-eastern edge of town, the colliery began operations in 1898 and was typical of the mines in the area. At the height of its operations it employed close on a thousand men and during its working life it saw the occasional strike and once, in 1916, thirteen men were lost in an explosion. The mine was closed in 1981 but now functions as a museum, a part of the burgeoning heritage industry sweeping through Northumberland. Through the colourful exhibits droves of schoolchildren tramp. On display too are some of the works by the Ashington Artists. This group, mostly comprised of miners, worked between 1934 and 1984 recording mining scenes and life in and around the pit villages.

The colliery, with its silent and rusting pit-head, takes its name from nearby Woodhorn, a little village to the east of Ashington. Woodhorn has a Saxon church much added to over the centuries to become a tableau of period styles. It was deconsecrated in 1973 and it too has become a museum. With the decline of the coal industry, Ashington and its surroundings lost their purpose and the local economy became depressed; the clean, new countryside has been their only compensation.

BEADNELL

This small fishing village, as with a number of the county's coastal sites, is best admired somewhere between January and March when driving rain and blustery winds keep tourism at bay. In this season the village remains unmolested by greasy chip shops, heaving caravan parks and the clogged ravines of traffic along the access roads.

Beadnell has a delightful and cosy harbour, sufficient for the cobles which row out in search of crab and lobster, and has the distinction of being the only west-facing harbour on the east coast. The harbour sits underneath the trunk-like limestone kilns of the eighteenth century, to one side of the sandy bay, which sweeps first to the west and then turns south to Snoot Point. In Saxon times there was a settlement here with a chapel dedicated to St Ebba, the sister of Oswald, the Christian king of Northumbria. Beadnell derives its name from the Low Ground by the Sea and it was here that Bedewine settled, on this attractive level beach with its flat hinterland. Somehow, Beadnell manages to retain its charm, due no doubt to its generous open expanses which manage to absorb the worst excesses of the wake of tourism.

RIDSDALE

This small village crawling up a long steep hill sits in an exposed and rather wild valley. Dere Street, the long straight road which carried the Roman legions north from York all the way up to the uncharted wilderness of Caledonia, passes this way. Just to the south of the village, undiscovered by footsore legionaries, there lay in Fourlaws Barrow until 1814 a splendid Bronze Age necklace of gold beads together with two bronze rings. Half a century later, William Armstrong began to manufacture iron here, taking advantage of the Ridsdale ironstone beds. It is here that the ruins of the rather castle-like engine-house can be seen. Inside there was a double-beam blowing engine which produced the air supply to the three blast furnaces. The nineteenth-century blast furnace needed iron ore of reasonable quality, good coking coal and limestone which acted as a flux to remove the slag and all were available in the neighbourhood. Armstrong invested a fair amount in this project, but by 1879 the works were discontinued and any machinery which could be transferred was dispatched to Armstrong's works in Elswick. Even so, in its brief life the ironworks supplied some of the iron used in the construction of Stephenson's high level bridge in Newcastle, the first to carry the railway over the Tyne.

GREY STREET, NEWCASTLE

Pevsner wrote in *Northumberland* that there were two things which distinguished Newcastle from other northern cities, its river and the team of Dobson the architect and Grainger the builder. 'In what way Grainger and Dobson form a special distinction need nowadays hardly be emphasized. They have given the whole centre of the old town a dignity and orderliness which even the twentieth-century advertising hysteria has not succeeding in destroying.' In many, but by no means all, respects this is still true. There were developments to come after Pevsner had written his book in 1957, which were to destroy something of the Dobson and Grainger achievement. Grey Street, which Pevsner describes as 'one of the best streets in England' curves gracefully along its length and plunges steeply down to the Quayside. The street was named in honour of the 2nd Earl Grey, Prime Minister and author of the 1832 Reform Bill which gave democracy a gentle onward shove. At the top of Grey Street is the Grey Monument, shown here, the city's version of Nelson's Column, which dwarfs its surroundings. On the base of the column is a commemoration to Grey's achievement which disgruntled rioters in the late nineteenth century were not above defacing. But one can see their point: the monument, if not somewhat out of proportion to its surroundings, may be slightly larger than Grey's achievement merited.

ALLENBANKS

The River Allen is perhaps the wildest in Northumberland and runs through often dramatic settings as it makes its final journey before joining the waters of the River South Tyne. Allenbanks lies a few miles to the west of Haydon Bridge along a length of mature woods of variety and grandeur. There are fine stands of oak and beech which, with their roots clinging desperately to the steeply rising banks, climb the valley sides. Through this gorge the peaty waters of the River Allen swirl along the last few miles of its length. Allenbanks was originally planted as a Georgian landscape for nearby Ridley Hall, once the home of the Ridleys, but subsequently acquired by the Bowes, and thereafter by the Bowes-Lyon family. In his book, *View of Northumberland*, written in 1827, A. Mackenzie describes the surroundings of Allenbanks as containing 'scenes at once beautiful, grand and romantic', which indeed they still are, but if anything wilder now than perhaps they once were. Such praise of the river gorge may also have overlooked erstwhile coal workings on the east bank. Depressions in the ground on this side attest to the presence of an exposed seam which once would have been the basis for these modest workings catering for local needs. Beyond here, on the east bank, there is a small tarn which has become a favourite haunt of several species of duck. The woods of the Allenbanks are alive with wildlife too: roe deer, red squirrel and an abundance of woodland birds. From the hill-top above the east bank, Hadrian's Wall can be seen in the distance.

NORTH SHIELDS

When the passenger traffic rolls off the Scandinavian ferry and joins the main road, this spectacle of urban geometry will greet the occupants' hungry eyes. From behind their cars' tinted windows, they can marvel at this vibrant feature of north-east culture – the allotment. Vital to the nurturing of leeks and pigeons, camaraderie and politics, it began its journey through history during the lean years of the Second World War. The 'Dig For Victory' campaign began under a massive onslaught of propaganda. In 1942 alone, 10 million leaflets advocating the use of gardens and the creation of allotments to grow food were distributed around the country. By the end of 1939 there were already 815,000 allotments in use, increasing to 1.4 million in 1943. In the middle of the war a survey conducted among manual workers revealed that over half their number kept either an allotment or a garden. This was supplemented by 6,900 pig clubs, and domestic hen-keepers were producing 25 per cent of known supplies of fresh eggs. After the war they kept on digging. Makeshift and sometimes chaotic, like weeds on a pavement, they poke up here and there across the city, almost an act of defiance to the onward rush of brick and tarmac.

EDLINGHAM

In an area chiefly moorland in character the hamlet of Edlingham lies in a narrow green vale. People have lived here since earliest times, and nearby in the hills there are cup-and-ring-marked stones. To the west lies the Roman road known as the Devil's Causeway, which can still be traced running across the ridge and furrow fields of a later date.

The name of the hamlet is Anglo-Saxon for the homestead of the Eadwulf family, and is first mentioned in 737 as one of many villages given to the monks of Lindisfarne by King Ceowulf of Northumbria when he abdicated his throne in order to become a monk at Holy Island. The ruins of the large pele tower, Edlingham Castle, date from the twelfth century. It was held in the reign of Henry II by John, son of Walden, and later, around 1519, passed into the hands of the Swinburnes of Capheaton. The church near to the ruins dates from Saxon times and is dedicated to St John the Baptist. It probably began as a wooden structure, to be replaced later in stone and consecrated by Bishop Egred in 840. The present church, which stands on the same site, is Norman, but in any event Christian worship has been practised here for over a thousand years.

CULLERCOATS

In 1749 Cullercoats had the reputation of being the best fish market in the north of England. The cobles with their brown-red sails and names like *Amity*, *Gratitude*, *Cock Robin* and *Star of Peace*, added colour and grace to the grey swell and heaving skies. A century later when the superb station at adjacent Tynemouth was completed, Cullercoats became an increasingly fashionable watering-hole. It was popular too with artists like Birket Foster, H.H. Emmerson and the American Winslow Homer who painted the church of St George with its delicate spire built by the Duke of Northumberland in 1882. At one time though, Cullercoats was more than just a fishing village; it was a busy port exporting salt, grindstones and coal. A wagonway ran from Whitely collieries to the harbour, and for some odd reason one of the collieries in North Shields which couldn't load there, sent its coal by carts to Cullercoats from where it was shipped. The last clearance of salt from the port was aboard the *Fortune* from Whitby, which sailed in 1726 with a cargo of 21 tons. Faint traces of the salt pans can apparently still be seen.

Today Cullercoats is a quiet commuter town, its sands fill up on Bank Holidays and in the summer it becomes a brisk bucket-and-spade resort.

HAYDON BRIDGE

Throughout the towns and villages of the county, memorials to the First World War, like this one to the men of Haydon Bridge parish, bear mute testimony to the folly which laid waste a generation of young men. Many of them appear as bleak as the events they recall, and with sad irony quite a few of them were dismantled during the Second World War when invasion fears were real enough, and efforts were made to remove signs which could identify places. By August 1916, two years into the war, the number of dead was estimated at 4.6 million. According to some sources, this number was double the total of those killed in the Crimean War, the American Civil War, the three Prussian Wars, the Boer War, the Russo-Japanese War and the Balkan War. In 1919, the overall losses of the First World War were put between 10 and 13 million.

The sheer scale of losses must have been largely the result of the ability of factories to mass-produce weapons and of a transport system able to deliver both men and munitions into the theatre of war. Northumberland played a large part in making this possible. It was George Stephenson who built the first successful locomotive and who, with his son Robert, established a locomotive works on the Forth Banks behind what is now Newcastle Central Station. There was, too, William Armstrong who built up an armaments empire to rival that of Krupps of Essen. The great engineering works of the region which produced ships, guns and trains and which brought livelihood to thousands with perverse symmetry also provided the means to send thousands more to their deaths.

HEXHAMSHIRE COMMON

Here, near to Blanchland and the border with County Durham, the common is less exposed. The River Derwent travels the border, but on the tops of both sides of the leafy river valley the moorland has scant protection from the elements. On a clear day there is good visibility, but for weeks on end in the winter months the common is often shrouded in mist or subject to bitter winds.

Blanchland occupies the site of an abbey to the Blessed Virgin, founded in 1175 by Walter de Bolbeck, the lord of the manor, for twelve Premonstratensian canons, missionary monks of St Norbert's severe rule. The colour of their habit meant they became known as the 'white canons' and it is from this that Blanchland may also take its name. Even this out of the way spot did not deter raiding parties from Scotland. A group of marauders, on their way to sack the abbey, got lost in the mists on Dead Friars Hill, only to be guided in by the bells, which proved fatal for the monks. Edward III passed through Blanchland in 1327, leaving Durham with an army of 60,000 men in search of the Scots whom he never found. After the Dissolution, Blanchland came into the possession of the Forsters, who also owned Bamburgh, and who used it for hunting. In those days there were plenty of stags up on the surrounding moors.

HEXHAM

Hexham has many fine shops but this one is in a class of its own. It isn't bright with neon and it isn't garish with advertising. It has no special offers, no orderly rows of uniformly scrubbed produce and it has no piped music. In fact, there is nothing much to compare it with modern shopping. Its dark, cluttered interior, though, is rich with atmosphere, one where Time has stopped fifty years ago. Produce has to be dug out of an assortment of sacks and boxes, then laboriously weighed and the totals added up, as if the whole process was some sort of exotic ritual which demanded no consciousness of time passing.

As with many of Northumberland's older towns, Hexham has a colourful and bloody past. Perched on the lower slopes of the Tyne valley, it has the river running at its feet. Hexham became a busy market-place and a focal point for the surrounding area, a role which it has played for thirteen centuries. In 674 Queen Ethelreda gave her spiritual advisor, St Wilfrid, land in Hexham on which to build a church. Wilfrid, who had trained under St Aidan on Lindisfarne, had lofty ambitions and was quick to establish a monastery to serve the church. However, both were sacked in 875 by the Danes and only the crypt survived of what, according to the chronicles of the period, was considered to be the finest church in England. The church was eventually rebuilt after two centuries of ruin when in 1113 Thomas II, Archbishop of York undertook the work. But this one only lasted until 1296 when, on this occasion, it was the Scots who sacked the town, including the school which reportedly had two hundred pupils inside even as it was burning. The following year it was the turn of William Wallace to finish off what the Scots had left behind. If the people of Hexham thought they were to be spared further depredations, they were wrong. The Scots were back again by 1312 and for the next six years Hexham was repeatedly ravaged by marauding Scots; and to make matters worse Tynedale was in the grip of famine, which added considerably to the desolation. After David of Scotland had plundered the church in 1346 Hexham was relatively calm for more than a century until its involvement in the Wars of the Roses when a battle was fought on Hexham levels about 3 kilometres to the south-east of the town in 1464. The Yorkists under Montacute defeated the Lancastrians under the Duke of Somerset, who was captured and beheaded. The next event to throw Hexham into turmoil came when Henry VIII called for the Dissolution of the Monasteries and the canons of Hexham rose up in armed revolt which was swiftly crushed by the Duke of Norfolk in 1536. Hexham's last disturbance came in 1761 when rioting miners, objecting to recruitment into the local militia, were involved in a brawl which left 50 dead and 300 injured.

THE LIT. AND PHIL., NEWCASTLE

The Literary and Philosophical Society was founded in 1793 as a forum for the exchange and debate of ideas and developments in literature and science. It had the social function of a club, providing a way for people to meet both formally and informally. Its present purpose-built site dates from 1825 and reflects the confidence of the Victorian Age. The entrance hall with its lofty proportions, and wide-sweeping staircase adorned with statues and paintings of erstwhile local notables, would comfortably accommodate a modern family home. Such grandeur also reflects Victorian self-importance but these were heady times. Tyneside was at the forefront of the invention and development of the railway, it was the birthplace of big bridges, big ships and big guns. The sheer scale of its engineering dwarfed everything which had come before and most of what has come along since. When Edison was busy in America, Joseph Swan was showing off his incandescent electric lamp in the Lit. and Phil. Mosley Street was the first street in the world to have electric light. The library was a repository of knowledge and of enlightenment; its volumes embraced the archaic as well as the arcane, the empiric and the eclectic. A glowing temple of achievement, the Lit. and Phil. represented what was noble about civilization, it was state-of-the-art and it was smug. Its perfection was left untampered, and while outside the world moved on, indoors its modernity gradually fossilized into splendid anachronism. That it functions at all must now be cause for wonder.

RIDLEY COMMON

In the upper dales and hills of Northumberland, the earliest method of farming would have involved seasonal migration, as may well have been the case here on Ridley Common above the Whitfield valley and the Staward gorge. Animals would be taken to the uplands to be grazed on the moors in the warmer months and the shepherds stayed with them. At the close of the sixteenth century a visitor to Redesdale, several miles to the east of here in upper north Tynedale, observed and recorded this practice.

> Here every way round about in the wasts as they term them you may see as it were the ancient nomads, a martiall kinde of men, who from the moneth of Aprill unto August, lye out scattering and summering with their catell in little cottages which they call shealings.

Even in the uplands, fresh pasture was not readily available. Often the land was too wet and the sheep didn't do well at all in this environment. Conditions only began to improve towards the end of the eighteenth century when landowners and farmers alike gradually introduced drainage and began to develop more resilient strains of sheep. Hill farms could then be established on a permanent basis as was probably the case with the farmstead The Steel, which is adjacent to this scene. Before this more permanent settling of the uplands there were few other activities in these parts. However, as Frank Atkinson in his book *Life and Traditions in Northumberland and Durham* (1977), pointed out, 'The only other evidence of human activities are some nineteenth-century coal mines, a few earlier bell pits, small quarries, turburaries (for peat-getting), illicit whisky stills and, from the early nineteenth century, shooting-butts.' Next to Ridley Common is the larger Plenmeller Common which today has a big open-cast coal-mining operation but still manages to function as a grouse moor.

CHIPCHASE ESTATE

During the troubled and uncertain years of Border warfare which spanned three centuries, Northumberland developed the defensive architecture for which it is famous. Fortified homes, farms and castles embraced several styles according to the means of those who could afford to build anything of consequence at all. For the poor, the option, if there was one, was to build for shelter and take chances on their dwellings standing up to anything worse than a thunderstorm. During the Border clashes these flimsy homes were frequently burnt to the ground.

Even after the Border was settled, there was still considerable lawlessness in Tynedale and Redesdale. There was widespread poaching, the rustling of sheep and cattle, and there was the illicit manufacture of whisky for which people on either side of the Border had acquired a taste. It took some time before the countryside gradually became more civilized and landlords could turn their attention once more to improving their estates. The old feudal system had become less workable, leading to landlords turning out some of their tenants to make way for new developments such as coal-mining, the production of wool or the growing of grain. At the same time, considerable importance was attached to the preservation of their traditional sporting rights. The new wealth generated by enclosure and improved agriculture or by coal-mining, facilitated this but sporting estates were, where possible, income-producing as well. Water bailiffs and gamekeepers were widely employed to combat the rampant poaching as well as to develop and maintain estates for field sports. Chipchase, for example, has both shooting and fishing and boasts one of the county's most attractive settings. Here the River Tyne loops through wide bends where sometimes oystercatchers wheel and dive above the waters in a display of formation flying, joined by cormorants who fish here too. Both banks are flanked by a thick belt of trees which gradually thin out through the parkland of Nunick on the north bank and Chipchase on the south bank.

THE ROMAN WALL, BLACKCARTS

This section of the Roman Wall is an area of the county where Roman ruins are abundant and where the Wall parallels the Military Road. General Wade, who constructed the Military Road in order to deal with recalcitrant Jacobites, very sensibly plundered the Wall of its stone to build his own road since a plentiful and accessible supply was on hand. This was equally true of the farms in the Wall's vicinity, many of which were built from stones lifted from the long defunct Wall and put to better use. Wade's road was built between 1752 and 1757, just three years less than the eight it took to build the Wall and fittingly Wade, who was probably the best road builder to reach the county since Roman times, used the Roman technology to further his own. Both the road and the Wall were inspired by military purpose though of course the Wall was a much more complex strategic asset. It was built to a width of 3 metres and to a height of 5 metres and was garrisoned with a dozen forts and numerous milecastles. The whole project was costly and labour-intensive and its secondary purpose may have been to keep the legions occupied. In any event it was an effective deterrent to keep barbarians out of the Empire and for close on 300 years served as the northern frontier of Rome. Additionally, just south of the Wall a vallum was dug, a spacious ditch which marked the rear of the military zone and controlled frontier traffic. To the north of the Wall a deep v-shaped ditch was dug effectively to heighten the defences and frustrate attack. The Wall, which was manned by auxiliaries from all over Europe rather than by legionaries from Rome itself, probably had a strength of ten thousand troops. The beauty of its structure was that aside from its obvious psychological deterrence, it was actually conceived as much for attack as for defence. Military strategy usually abhors monolithic defences which sooner or later can be breached, but the Wall was designed for speedy access along its length and for the rapid deployment of forces sent out from its forts to repel invaders. These would be sent north from the Wall in event of attack, to encircle the enemy and pin it down in the ditches below the Wall.

KIELDER

The First World War imposed a great strain on the nation's timber resources, over 250,000 hectares of woodland being felled. After the war the Forestry Act of 1919 brought the Forestry Commission into being to grow and manage state forests, help care for private woodlands and undertake research. Kielder Forest began with planting at Smales Farm in 1926, 45 acres leased at two shillings per acre. In 1930, with the death of the 8th Duke of Northumberland, Kielder Estate was sold off to pay death duties and by 1932 it had passed into the hands of the Forestry Commission. Thereafter expansion was rapid, with half the forest being planted between 1945 and 1960, so that it now covers an area of 62,000 hectares of which 50,000 are planted. The forest spreads into Cumbria and reaches up to the Scottish border. It also embraces Kielder Water, the largest man-made reservoir in northern Europe.

There are some 150 million standing trees here, of which 75 per cent are Sitka Spruce, the only species which actually thrives in this area. Norway Spruce and Lodgepole Pine and a very few Scots Pine make up the rest. At present 3 per cent of the forest is hardwood; the Commission is trying to increase this to 10 per cent by the end of the century. Kielder lies inside the National Park so the Forestry Commission as well as the Countryside Commission are seeking to conserve and improve wildlife habitats, to develop the forest, along with Kielder Water, for recreational use, and to improve the design of the forest. It has to be said that the artificial look to both the reservoir and the forest will probably not disappear for a very long time, but then they are industrial sites which might have looked a lot worse. Within the forest, though, there is still room for sixteen Sites of Special Scientific Interest and a protected habitat for red squirrels and otters, and there are not so many places where either species can easily survive these days.

BLYTH

The rotting hulks of a Soviet submarine and a freighter lie abandoned in the mud of a breaker's yard in one corner of Blyth's harbour. The yard went out of business before the work of breaking up the ships had been completed. For the present they are a lingering souvenir to the collapse of an empire, unnoticed and forgotten. This wasn't the first time submarines had slunk into Blyth's safe and spacious harbour. It has an outlet to the south-east which made it accessible even to boats under sail. During the Second World War, the harbour served as a base for submarines and much of it was fortified, with substantial gun emplacements and look-out posts surrounding the town. The submarines would have cruised nearly a mile out to sea before they left behind the harbour's two piers.

There is no longer a naval base here, though at one time there was a shipyard which turned out the odd boat for the Navy. The second *Ark Royal* was constructed by Blyth's shipbuilders. Another activity which animated the harbour dates back to medieval times when the first harbour existed. Several of the monasteries maintained salt pans on the shore and there are records which indicate that salt was first exported in 1208. Both wood and coal were used as fuel to evaporate the sea water in the salt pans.

ALNMOUTH

The origins of Alnmouth date back to the seventh century when the village was a focus for early Christian activity, and it was here, according to the Venerable Bede, that the great Synod was held at which Cuthbert was chosen to be the bishop of Lindisfarne in 684. A number of Saxon artefacts have been discovered here, particularly a carved cross which was dug up on Church Hill in 1789. It was 0.86 metres high and bore the inscription '*Myredeh meh wo*' – Myredeh me wrought – and along one edge the name Eadwulf appears, suggesting that it was carved to commemorate the death of the king who was slain at Bamburgh.

The town is perched on a narrow spit of land, caught between the estuary of the Aln and the North Sea. Church Hill, a place of fine views, was the site of the old Saxon church dedicated to St Waleric and equally of the Norman one devoted to St John the Baptist. This latter was destroyed when on Christmas Day in 1806 a severe gale knocked it down. In the fourteenth century the ships of 'Alemouth', as it was then known, were frequently called upon to defend the kingdom and it served as well as the port for Alnwick. In the eighteenth and early nineteenth century Alemouth was a thriving port, chiefly exporting corn, which was stored in large granaries. It also received imports from London, Holland and Norway, and even built ships; one at least, of 300 tons, is known to have been launched here.

During the war with France in the eighteenth century several skirmishes took place off the coast of Alnmouth but only one cannon was fired at the town, and that in 1779 by an American buccaneer, Paul Jones, who missed the old church but demolished a farmhouse with the 68-pound ball. A little earlier, when John Wesley visited Alnmouth in 1748, he wrote of it as 'a small seaport famous for all kinds of wickedness', a long way from the genteel resort that it has long since become. Here on the beach beyond the golf links which separate it from the town, there is the occasional row of anti-tank blocks which were part of Northumberland's coastal defences during the Second World War.

ELLINGTON

The shafts of Ellington Colliery were first sunk between 1910 and 1913 and the seams were worked for the next forty years until a major refurbishment was needed in the mid-fifties. As a result of this the Lynemouth and the Ellington collieries were connected underground by the Lynemouth Bewick drift and it was from here that the output of both collieries was mined. The two pits were finally merged in 1983, partly because of the increasing rationalization of coal-mining and partly because new reserves had been discovered but these were out to sea, almost 10 kilometres from the coast. There is currently an annual output of 2 million tonnes of coal, which on arrival at the colliery is carried by a covered conveyor belt to the nearby coal preparation plant. When it arrives here, the coal is washed and screened and divided up into two halves. One half is then carried on a brief journey by another conveyor to the Alcan smelter, while the other half is delivered to a number of power stations around the country. The whole operation is discreet, the miners are rarely to be seen, everything is carefully screened off from view, and gone is the usual paraphernalia which spells out mining to the casual passer-by. There are of course the vast heaps of coal outside the preparation plant waiting to be processed, but these too are hidden from the casual gaze.

In all some 1500 people are employed in the Ellington operation; now and again their numbers are trimmed as improved technology and efficiency reduce the labour required for this operation. The reserves though are plentiful and as yet there has been no decline in demand. Off the back of this smooth machine-led mining process, there is still room for the odd coalie or two, like the men in this scene, to gather pickings for their own domestic use.

COALCLEUGH

All but abandoned, Coalcleugh is perched in a cleft of upland moor where the River West Allen is no more than a burn. Reputedly, it was once the highest village in England but now only a few ruins remain. They are a reminder of its emptiness, that up here there is nothing much but the sky and the wind, the one at times as menacing as the other is unrelenting. It seems to have been bypassed by the twentieth century but there has been little enough reason for its intrusion. A few hill farmers graze sheep on the moor, and in season, a few guns come up here for the grouse but otherwise there is little to disturb its peace.

What first brought people here when nothing else would, was the lead-mining. Such enterprise in Northumberland can be traced back to the Roman occupation and already by the reign of Henry I there were complaints about miners destroying the woodland in the Allendales. By the eighteenth century the industry was flourishing, and Coalcleugh boasted the first underground horse-drawn wagonway, which ran for a mile. In his book *The Northumbrian Uplands* (1989), Geoffrey N. Wright gives a fascinating description of mining techniques and recounts how the levels and shafts in the upland valleys of the rivers Allen yielded in excess of a quarter of a million tons of lead concentrates between 1729 and 1896. The decline of lead-mining, and none is now mined in the county, was because of the falling price, from around £32 per ton in 1850 to £13 per ton by the end of the century, as a result of competition.

SIMONSIDE

Simonside is a heather covered sandstone ridge lying to the south-west of Rothbury. From its ridges are fine views to the Cheviot massif in the north, and south towards Selby's Cove. The presence of heather is often taken for granted hereabouts because of the well-drained sandstone uplands, but sheep-grazing at the expense of grouse management can lead to sparser cover as is the case on the granite in the heart of the Cheviots.

In the eighteenth and nineteenth centuries heather moors were greatly extended by wealthy landowners to provide better grazing as well as for sport. The finest moors are those where some degree of management is practised. Young heather shoots are the staple diet of red grouse, so the burning of patches of heather each year helps to establish a variety of different aged heather to provide cover for nesting and to ensure a constant supply of food. The rotation of a well managed moor varies between seven and fifteen years, which can lead to up to 300 grouse per square mile. On the Simonside hills, the expanses of heather are broken up by crags, cleughs and bogs and offer a habitat which attracts meadow pipits, golden plovers and curlews. During late summer bee-keepers bring their hives up to profit from the rich harvest of nectar and pollen. In the clumps of older, deeper heather, lurk the ground-nesting merlins, and as long as there are plenty of pipits about they are more than content.

NORTH SHIELDS

In recent years North Shields has undergone a major programme of reconstruction and it still seems to be reeling from the shock of it. It is hard to tell if it will recover, but where changes have been wrought, some of what has gone up looks more bleakly functional than what was pulled down. Its new streets, glossy with cloned homes and concrete precincts, now surround in forlorn antipathy the sad carcasses of the few fine old buildings which remain standing. These once imposed discipline and gravitas to what was mostly a sprawling maze of predominantly mean streets. At one time the back-to-back terraces spilled down on to the steep banks of the Tyne; grimy and dour they only ever shone in the rain, but they were rich in character and somehow held out the promise of adventure. A street like this one on the east side of the Shields, though more prosperous, faintly echoes the style of those erstwhile streets.

The same streets produced a variety of characters, one of the earliest of whom was Ralph Gardner, a man imprisoned and persecuted for his beliefs. He vigorously contested the rights of brewers and other merchants to monopolize the markets of the Tyne. In 1655 he published *England's grievance discovered in relation to the Coal Trade*. Later sons of the Shields included John Dobson the distinguished architect and Myles Birket Foster the landscape artist. Stan Laurel was born here in Dockwray Square, now renamed after him, and replete with a statue (of him) in his typical head-scratching posture gazing out across the Tyne.

NEWBIGGIN-BY-THE-SEA

In 1878, when a gang of workmen were digging a cutting to the seashore for a sewerage outlet, three Bronze Age spearheads were uncovered here, as too was a bed of peat, 2 metres under the sand, embedded with tree trunks and hazelnuts. Three thousand years ago Northumberland, like much of the rest of England, was one great forest and the population probably not much above a few hundred who wandered around the countryside. No other Bronze Age traces have been found here but it is known that there was a Saxon settlement called South Wallerick. Inevitably, this was sacked by the Danes in 875, and the original chapel of ease, erected by the monks of Lindisfarne, was lost. By 1203, Newbiggin-by-the-Sea was of sufficient importance to be granted a fair and a market charter. Throughout the Middle Ages, Newbiggin was a port of some consequence and it had a pier on the north side of the harbour as early as 1352. Its main function was the export of large quantities of corn, though occasionally it had other tasks to perform. During the wars of Edward II with Scotland, the port was required to furnish a naval vessel and the king himself tarried here for three days on his way to lay siege to Berwick. The magnificent sweep of the bay, caught between two rocky promontories, is still animated by a few fishing cobles which are dragged across the sands with tractors before they are launched.

On the headland is the ancient church of St Bartholomew which has long served as a reference for passing ships. Its extensive graveyards, some with curious epitaphs, stretch westwards from the church. On the seaward side, erosion led to the desecration of several tombs and now and again fragments of human bones can be scuffed up in the sands.

THE QUAYSIDE, NEWCASTLE

The quayside is lent a certain grandeur by the imposing structure of the Tyne bridge, which provided the model for Sydney harbour bridge in Australia. It was opened by George V in 1928 and named after him, though rarely called that by locals. On the south bank the solid block of the Baltic flour mills provides the breeding grounds for a few hundred kittiwakes.

The quayside grew out of docks and piers on the river front, into which large quantities of ballast were dumped by ships before loading, eventually creating a strip of land on which the quays now stand. The land was used for building homes, notably for those involved in some way with shipping – anyone from merchants to keelmen – though by the nineteenth century these had given way to warehousing and industry. In 1854, however, a fire broke out in Newcastle's wife – Gateshead – in Wilson's Worsted Manufactory, which was stuffed to the gills with wool. Within an hour the building was gutted. Next door, the Bertram and Spenser warehouse, which was about 100 metres long and filled, among other things, with 170 tons of manganese, 800 tons of lead, 130 tons of nitrate of soda, arsenic, brimstone, guano and naphtha, went up like a Guy Fawkes of spectacular but lethal proportions. Thousands turned out to watch on both sides of the river and then the warehouse blew up with much the same effect as a magazine exploding. Windows and gaslights on both sides of the river blew out, molten embers landed on the timber ships moored along the quayside, setting them alight, roofs were crushed by the tons of falling debris, and people on both sides of the river were mown down by the shrapnel generated by the explosion and fragments from the 200 tons of iron stored in the warehouse. By the morning the fire had spread 110 metres along the quayside and it burned for two days before it was finally put out. In his engaging study *Waters of Tyne* (1991), T.H. Rowland provides a graphic account of the fire and its aftermath.

NEWCASTLE

The city spreads out over a number of valleys and hills on the north bank of the Tyne. The Romans were the first to put a bridge over the river. At that time, the Tyne was much wider than it is now, and it is thought that the Romans could have crossed it on foot at low tide, a factor which would have helped Hadrian when the bridge was built around AD 120 and called Pons Aelius after his family. The bridge was probably situated more or less where the swing bridge now crosses the river. The Romans provided a fort to guard the bridge and this is thought to have stood on the same site where in 1080 Robert Curthose, eldest son of William the Conqueror, established a new stronghold. After a period in Scottish hands, this stronghold was rebuilt by Henry II, and it was from the new castle, effectively, that the town took its name and its beginning.

The site offers strategic views of the river which for the Romans was important as they were the first to develop its potential for trade; it was also the start of the frontier zone and it was along the river that their logistics came. Subsequently, it remained a frontier zone between the English and the Scots, reflected in the presence of its thirteenth-century city walls; it was after all the area's main urban settlement, a long way from the seat of power in the south, and had therefore to assume a role of surrogate on the northern frontier. It was coal, however, which was largely responsible for the substantial growth and wealth of the city and was to pave the way for its great engineering projects which reached their zenith in the early part of this century.

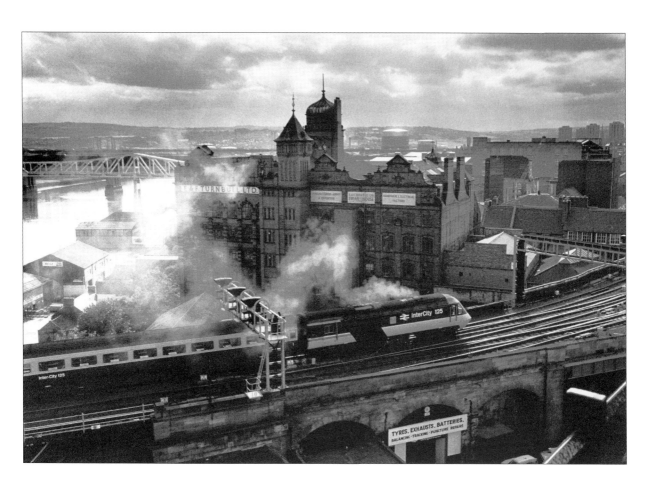

NORTH SHIELDS

At its east end North Shields merges into Tynemouth where the river finally meets the sea. It is North Shields, or on the south bank, South Shields, though, which offers the first safe anchorages. The Old High Light of 1727 and the High Light of 1808 were built above the fish quays to guide vessels in. Many never made it; the waters were notorious for their treachery and there were several disasters, notably on Black Middens reef, until the piers were eventually built – itself an arduous challenge. Their completion did help to reduce disasters and afford shipping greater protection.

Since Roman times there has been a steady stream of shipping passing in and out of the Tyne. The Romans brought provisions in this way, destined for the Wall down-river at Wallsend. Anglo-Saxons came first as raiders then as settlers and provided the transport for the innumerable monks and nuns, some of whom were based at Jarrow or Tynemouth. By medieval times the river was bustling with merchant vessels and warships and by the time of the Spanish Armada, Tynemouth was virtually a fortress, and it was to be equally busy during the Napoleonic Wars, the Civil War and the Jacobite rebellions.

North Shields was rather more humble and the shiels on the banks of the river were for fishermen, many of whom were catering for the needs of the priory at Tynemouth and the Church in general. The heyday of North Shields as a fishing community peaked early in the twentieth century when there were some seventy steam trawlers landing 20,000 tons of herrings annually. The industry is now a shadow of what it once was, caused as much as anything by over-fishing, though not by any means just by local fishermen.

THE FISH QUAY, NORTH SHIELDS

Fishing began at the mouth of the Pow burn as early as 1225 when the shiels were first put up for the inshore fishermen catching haddock and codling using mussels for bait. There were already fish ponds kept by the monks of neighbouring Tynemouth, but this new supply was welcomed. The monks brought the fishermen within their protection and applied to them the trading privileges granted by Richard I, which effectively freed them from interference from Newcastle. By 1290 there were two hundred shielings and North Shields was becoming an established community and causing the freemen of Newcastle grave concern. They complained in Parliament and called, successfully, for the destruction of the North Shields settlement on the basis that the king's toll on herring, cod and garfish was under threat from the fishermen. Their jetties and mussel-beds were broken up. By 1442 this turn of fortune had been reversed, with the priory able to muster a fleet of sixteen fishing boats able to make the journey to Iceland. Once again the freemen of Newcastle complained that they thought it somewhat excessive that sixteen monks had sixteen boats landing catch solely for their benefit. By the sixteenth century, the pendulum had swung again; the herring shoals had departed, and the Dissolution of the Monasteries had led to the departure of the monks. The fishermen soon followed.

The fish quay dates from 1874. By then the shoals and the boats were back, and in addition a rail link to Newcastle allowed the fish to reach markets in London. The busy season ran through June into July when the herring shoals were off the Tyne.

NETHERWITTON

Sheltered by steep ridges to the north and south as well as by the Newpark and Oldpark Woods, the village of Netherwitton lies in the angle formed by the River Font and the Ewesley burn. At one time the village was known as Witton-by-the-Waters, doubtless because of the confluence which once served the mill dam. Somewhere among the gardens of Netherwitton, a stone cross with 1698 inscribed upon it recalls the period when the village was Catholic. Near to where an old bridge scans the Font is an erstwhile woollen mill, originally built for the manufacture of cotton in a venture which was never successful. Beyond the mill, hidden among the trees, is the church of St Giles, with next to the pulpit a full-length figure of a woman carved in stone, discovered when the foundations of the north wall of the nave were dug.

Netherwitton Hall, whose gardens adjoin the church on one side, became the seat of the Trevelyan family when the estate passed to them by marriage with the Thorntons. Roger Thornton, a merchant of Newcastle, had bought the manor of Witton in 1405 and built a castle here which is said to have stood in the grounds of the present hall. In the summer of 1651 Oliver Cromwell brought his army to Netherwitton, and there quartered them for a night. His army consisted of nine foot regiments, two regiments of dragoons and Cromwell's horseguards. According to tradition, Netherwitton was also the hiding place of Lord Lovat, who hid in the priest's hole so common to Catholic houses of the time and remained here from the time of the Battle of Culloden until his eventual capture.

BRIZLEE WOOD

Just inside the south side of Hulne Park, the walled estate of the Dukes of Northumberland, is Brizlee Wood, a NATO installation and a legacy of the Cold War. It stands on the uplands overlooking Alnwick in the valley below; its large dishes were part of a web of NATO communication links which stretched across Europe. For many years Brizlee Wood served as a relay for satellite signals but it was decommissioned in 1990. The dishes will be dismantled, but for the present they remain dominating the skyline for miles around, sometimes rendered spookily dramatic by leaden skies or when glimpsed momentarily through a gap in swirling mists. Outwardly they are barely different from other incongruous bits of technology which crop up here and there on the county's landscape, but for those who read their symbolism, the very presence of Brizlee Wood was disturbing; it spoke of fragile peace, of covert wars and of the arms race. Other, earlier, chapters of military history lie within sight of Brizlee Wood, principally the castles of Bamburgh, Dunstanburgh and Warkworth. It was because of the impressive views that Hugh, the first Duke of Northumberland, had a folly built on neighbouring Brizlee Hill in 1871 by the prolific Robert Adam, who gothicized Alnwick Castle only to have the larger part of his work ripped up by the fourth duke a hundred years later. The folly was also positioned so that the setting of Hulne Park could be enjoyed and there is an inscription on the tower itself which boasts of Hugh's achievement in creating Hulne Park. Around the hilltop and beyond Brizlee Wood too are a number of ancient Celtic earthworks which may reflect the strategic position of the site.

OLD BEWICK

Given the importance of bees to the early economy of the county, it is hardly surprising that there are many place names associated with them. Old Bewick means the old bee farm. Before sugar was imported into Britain, honey was a valuable commodity since it provided one of the few sources of sweetening. Beeswax was also widely used in the home and in churches, and when tithes were assessed, they applied as much to bees as to farm animals. Even as late as the mid-nineteenth century the records of the Tithe Commissioners show that levies were still imposed on beehives.

The manor here was held in Saxon and Norman times under the king's castle at Bamburgh and formed part of the dowry of Matilda, the daughter of King Malcolm of Scotland, when she married Henry I. In turn it was given by her to the monks of Tynemouth who were responsible for the building of the church between 1110 and 1120. Alongside the attractive church with its neatly kept graveyard, runs the tiny Kirk burn which spills into the River Breamish. A little further on at Bewick bridge, a graceful single-arch of weathered stone, the Breamish becomes the Till and winds its way through a landscape which owes much to eighteenth- and nineteenth-century enclosures. It is a part of Northumberland rich with the legacy of Iron Age Celts and above the village to the east is Bewick hill which is crowned with a fine example of a Celtic hill fortress. The defences, which included four ramparts and deep ditches which surrounded the circular huts, would have been used in times of crisis. Associated with Bewick camp are a nearby series of blocks of sandstone which are carved with concentric circles still faintly discernible after twenty or thirty centuries. Sitting atop the ramparts on either side of the hill are two pill-boxes which were hastily constructed during the Second World War to maintain defendable positions in the event of invasion. From this hill there are superb views overlooking Hedgeley moor and to the west the swell of the Cheviots beckons.

INGOE

The hamlet of Ingoe is set in countryside full of gentle rural attractions. Its slightly elevated position affords clear views for miles around, a fact which may help explain why the Romans maintained outposts here. Ingoe, which means the meadow on the hill, is nothing more than a row of cottages, set apart from a minor road that twists through the countryside, linking up a few scattered farms. But its antiquity is older than Rome as the presence of the nearby Warrior Stone suggests. It stands a metre or more high in a sloping meadow within sight of the cottages and slightly beyond Sandywayhead Farm, with the spread of Northumberland at its best unfurling before it. Some theorists like to suggest that such standing stones as this may be among the oldest monuments in the world and among the most remarkable. They hold the view that in some way their construction, which in places must have needed considerable ingenuity as well as effort, was bound up with an advanced understanding of mathematics and astronomy, so far ahead of its time that it upsets scientific orthodoxy about what is believed of neolithic peoples. They cite the common unit of measurement, the megalithic yard, of 2.72 feet, with which the Stone Age builders constructed circles, ellipses and other shapes with a knowledge previously credited to Pythagoras whose discoveries were made more than a thousand years later. Even worse, it was thought that their constructions must have implied a knowledge of Π (pi) at least two millennia before it was first known to have been recorded. Needless to say, the debate continues to excite the imagination for there is still very little known about the culture of the people who used and built these monuments. The county has many examples which have adorned the landscape for the past thirty centuries or more and as Daniel Defoe remarked of them, summing up the attitude of the eighteenth century if not the twentieth, 'all that can be learn'd of them is, that there they are'.

HIGH STAWARD

Enclosure began to make its mark on the landscape of Northumberland from the seventeenth century and gained momentum in the eighteenth century and continued as late as the middle of the nineteenth century. In the valleys and lower slopes, the new fields were often imprisoned by hedges, set on earth mounds created by digging ditches. The most popular hedge was made from hawthorn because not only did this grow quickly, but it was also stockproof if properly maintained. Some farmers cut their hedges when young and then trimmed them annually, whereas others allowed the hawthorns to mature for nine or ten years before rotating them. The latter method was the more popular in the county, chiefly because it was found more attractive and there was little difference in cost between the two. On the higher slopes, drystone walls were preferred, though at the time many thought that they were unnatural and inclined to carve up the hillsides with regimented geometry. They were, however, the obvious solution and an abundance of stones was nearly always at hand from a plethora of small quarries and from plundered prehistoric monuments. The skill of these wall builders went unnoticed in their own lifetime, perhaps no one imagined they would last as well as they did, but nowadays, it is almost impossible to maintain them effectively without cash grants to subsidize such labour-intensive work. More to the point, they do not always deter sheep from climbing over them. High Staward, which lies between Catton and Whitfield, provides on these slopes a maze of fields interlaced with drystone walls before they reach the moor which cuts Hexham off from Catton and Allendale.

GUNNERTON

Most history about the Bronze Age in the county has come from the chance discovery of burial sites, often when some farm machine has dislodged the capstone of a cist in which human remains, along with some valued or useful object, are concealed. The placing of objects in the burial chamber was no doubt connected to the belief in an afterlife. At Short Moor Farm, which lies just beyond the village here, a burial site revealed the remains of a man who had been 2 metres tall, aged between thirty-five and forty-five years old and who had walked with a limp. His left leg had been broken, but despite an early infection had managed to heal. In neighbouring Barrasford a similar find was made, and it may well be that these are the remains of the first settlers in Tynedale.

The Gunnerton crags were also the almost impregnable stronghold of the old Celtic tribes. Two of their settlements lie either side of Gunnar Heugh, with massive ramparts and outlying circular guard chambers. The next strongholds came with the Normans but their hold on upper Tynedale was at best precarious and they probably did not reach here until the twelfth century during the reign of Henry I. Their occupation was based upon the construction of a line of motte and bailey castles along the North Tyne valley, stretching from Hexham via Gunnerton – where there was a motte – and Wark up to Bellingham.

Sir John Fenwicke who held the manor here also had a tower and stone house in the village, recorded in Henry VIII's survey of castles and fortifications in 1541.

BYWELL

Bywell is a rather curious but very charming village with two small churches, a castle, a rectory, a country house and one or two houses all caught in a sweeping bend of the Tyne. In Saxon times there were two estates here, hence the two churches, of St Peter and St Andrew, known as the White and the Black. In Norman times there were two baronies, those of Balliol and of Bolbec. The Balliols granted their church of St Peter to the Black monks at the monastery in Durham, while the church of St Andrew was given to the White monks of Blanchland. In medieval times there was a bustling community at Bywell comprised of various craftsmen and iron-workers, and the village ran two water corn mills and fished their salmon by damming the river. In 1464 Henry VI took refuge in the castle, whose construction had been begun some forty years earlier by Ralph Neville but was never completed save for the gatehouse and barmkin. Following the Revolt of the Northern Earls in 1569, the castle came into the jurisdiction of Elizabeth I. There followed a period of decline; its woods were chopped for timber, its red deer and the salmon were poached and the village no longer successfully functioned as a thriving and industrious community. In 1771 Bywell, along with several other places on the Tyne, was caught in the Great Flood and the village lost ten of its houses.

Bywell's present-day slumbers are rarely interrupted by anything more dramatic than the brief passage of the Tynedale Hunt as it canters through the village in pursuit of a fox making for the banks of the Tyne where the river swirls past the church of St Peter standing on a small promontory above.

HOLY ISLAND

When Edwin died he left Northumbria in ascendance over the southern kingdoms, but this did not last for long, and his successors faced many reversals fighting the British king Cadwallon and the Mercian prince Penda. Christianity was set back on course after Oswald defeated the heathens at the battle of Heavenfield, close to Hexham, in 634. One of his first acts after victory was to ask the Scottish elders to send a bishop from Iona, and they sent him Aidan, who was quick to establish an episcopal see on Holy Island. He didn't speak English and his sermons had to be translated so that the Northumbrian thanes could understand his teachings, but despite this, or possibly because of it, Christianity was quick to spread throughout the county and so gain a toehold in England. However, the power of Northumbria was to wane not just because of the rivalry with the Mercians and Scots, but because of successive Viking raids on Northumbria's coast. Holy Island was sacked and pillaged by the Danes in 793 and the monks were forced to leave, taking with them their illuminated manuscript of the Lindisfarne gospels and the corpse of St Cuthbert. Lindisfarne became a holy island for a second time when, in 1093, a priory was built as a branch of the monastery at Durham.

For up to eleven out of every twenty-four hours the sea cuts off Holy Island from the mainland, and when the tide is out the island becomes the tip of a vast peninsula of sand, the feeding ground of thousands of wildfowl and waders. Beyond the harbour, perched on a cone of rock is the sixteenth-century fort, redesigned by Lutyens in 1902.

ALNWICK

The former county town of Northumberland is dominated by the castle, once the strongest fortress on the English side of the border. Its imposing keep and ring of grey stone towers belie its humble beginnings as just another of the Norman strongholds established in the twelfth century as part of a damage limitation strategy against the devastating raids of the Scots. The de Vescis were the first barons but Henry, the first Lord Percy, who acquired it in 1309, greatly strengthened the defences of Alnwick. The Percys who already had lands in Sussex and Yorkshire were keen to augment their real estate in Northumberland, though in the end it was to prove hard won. Alnwick remained in the hands of the Percys until the death of the last Percy, the 11th Earl of Northumberland in 1670. The estate then passed by marriage to the Duke of Somerset and then, later still, by a second marriage to Sir Hugh Smithson, a canny Yorkshire baronet. He had the bright idea of changing his name to Percy and somehow he became the Earl of Northumberland in 1750 and, sixteen years later, managed to have this converted into a dukedom. The new Percys were back in business and are still in Alnwick today.

By the middle of the eighteenth century little was left of the original Norman castle, so Hugh transformed Alnwick Castle into a vast gothic palace to the design of Robert Adam and James Paine. A century later the whole thing was ripped apart and remodelled by the fourth duke, this time with an Italian flavour. The battlements of Alnwick though still retain the stone soldiers, once intended as some sort of threat to would-be marauders but which are curiously reminiscent of the toy soldiers that used to be found in Cornflakes packets. Surrounding the castle, both in the town and in the grounds of Hulne Park, are a number of buildings which reflect the history of the last millenium. Hulne Park was partly laid out by Capability Brown and Hugh, the first duke, took delight in dotting it with a number of ornamental buildings, like this one here which reflected his enthusiasm for the picturesque.

MONK WOOD

Monk Wood lies across the valley from Whitfield Hall, cut off by the River West Allen, in a setting of considerable charm. The wood reaches down to the river itself and, as it stretches westwards away from Whitfield, it follows the line of the river a while until it gives way to the fells beyond which reach up to Acton moor. Whitfield Hall which looks out to Monk Wood across a mature park, was granted by William the Lion, King of Scotland, to the canons of Hexham in the latter part of the twelfth century. After the dissolution of Hexham Abbey, Whitfield estate was purchased by the Whitfields and subsequently passed to the Ords. Writing his *View of Northumberland* in 1827, Mackenzie spoke warmly of Whitfield: 'It is altogether a lovely spot and appears like the garden of Eden in the midst of a wilderness.' The Hall was largely rebuilt towards the end of the eighteenth century by William Ord, who also made substantial improvements to the enclosures and plantations. At its east end the wood almost brushes up against the village of Whitfield, beyond which the valley narrows and its sides steepen and are covered with a profusion of trees.

WHITELY CHAPEL

The road south of Hexham climbs steeply up a long valley side which after a few kilo-metres levels out on a plateau criss-crossed with minor roads which reach farms and hamlets. Whitely Chapel is no more than a few cottages gathered around a cross-roads and these routes run out when they reach Burntridge Moor, Lilswood Moor or Blanchland Moor. Whitely Chapel lies as if in limbo between the desert and the sown; Hexhamshire Common cuts it off to the west and Slaley forest to the east, and to the south a bleak fell marks the frontier with County Durham. It was across Hexhamshire Common that the packhorses would ply back and forth carrying the lead ore from the mines of Allendale to the smelt mills, a task usually performed by small tenant farmers who leased their farms from the mining companies and used this work to boost their meagre incomes. The Broad Way was one of the routes which ran from Allenheads via Tedham Moss and Lilswood Moor and then through Whitely Chapel and on to the smelt mill at nearby Dukesfield. In *The Northumbrian Uplands* Geoffrey N. Wright cites a report produced in 1786 which describes the transport of ore:

> The Ore is carried from the Mines to the Mills entirely on Horseback; Galloways being employed, carrying two Pokes of Ore, each weighing 1 cwt, that is ⅛ of a Bing, consequently a Bing is carried by 4 Galloways.

Whitely Chapel takes its name from an oratory which existed here in medieval times and at some unrecorded date fell into ruin but was eventually rebuilt in the early part of the seventeenth century. It was the tradition of the Quakers in this area to hold their meetings on Chapel Hill and they were successful in gathering a gradually increasing number of participants so that the chapel had to be enlarged in 1695. Almost three hundred years later, Whitely Chapel can scarcely have grown, except for the tiny Methodist chapel which sits at the foot of the bank on which this little church stands.

CHIPCHASE

Chipchase was the hunting grounds of the lords of Prudhoe, the family of the Umfavilles who held it as a detached manor of the barony during the reign of Henry II. A small fort was erected to the south of the present castle to offer protection to Chipchase village, whose origin was Saxon and which survived until the eighteenth century. Chipchase passed by marriage to the Heron family so famous in Border history, and it was around this time that the pele tower was built. Sir George Heron, keeper of Tynedale and High Sheriff of Northumberland, was killed in one of the many clashes of the period, in 1575, in a fight known as the Raid of Redeswire. The Scots afterwards offered falcons to their prisoners, claiming that they were nobly treated, since while the English got live hawks, they only got dead herons. It was Cuthbert Heron who added the Jacobean manor house onto the pele tower in 1621, during the reign of James I, and it is reckoned to be the finest example of its kind in the county. The pele tower itself is also a very fine example of its type and ranks with Belsay as being the most impressive in the north. The tower measures about 15.5 metres by 10 metres and its battlements rose about 15 metres off the ground. In its day the pele tower was a very solid defence and in addition it had a basement with its own well. The basement was vaulted and powerfully built with walls 3 metres thick. It was designed to be self-contained and self-sufficient at times of crisis; the tower even had its own chapel room. The last of the Herons of Chipchase, Sir Harry, sold the estate towards the end of the seventeenth century.

River Allen

Just beyond the point where the East Allen joins the West Allen to become the River Allen is the Cupola Bridge. In the days of lead-mining, ore was brought down from Alston moor to the smelt mills at Whitfield, known as Cupola, and deriving their name from the Cupola type of 'reverberatory' furnace. Beyond the bridge, the river plunges into the Staward gorge and enters its most spectacular stretch. The waters are strewn with boulders and the banks rise cliff-like on either side, swathed in dense forest. W.J. Palmer, writing in *The Tyne and its Tributaries* in 1882, said of this setting that it had the characteristic 'of grand landscape scenery so well realised in the works of Turner and sometimes those of Martin. It may be, that Martin, whose birthplace is only two miles distant, received here early inspirations which afterward found expression in some of his highly popular pictures'.

Some way down the gorge, massive rocks form a natural lock, damming back the waters to form a deep and sombre pool by the name of Cyper's Linn, at the bottom of which lies a box of gold, possibly lost by monks as they crossed the erstwhile drawbridge here. Several unsuccessful attempts have been made to recover it, one of which was tragic. A local farmer managed to attach ropes to the box, in itself an extraordinary feat, and was hauling them up with his two oxen, Bran and Brock, when they lost their footing and all were plunged into the depths. An angler who has frequented the spot for years remembers one particularly fine summer when, the waters having dropped way beyond anything he had ever known, he saw the horns of the oxen as he was casting.

HOWICK HALL

Northumberland is littered with many fine country houses and while Howick is by no means the jewel in the crown as an architectural masterpiece, it is worthy on other counts. For one thing it has a splendid setting on the open coastal plain of north Northumberland and is barely 2 kilometres from the sea and only a few more from Craster and Dunstanburgh a little further up the coast. The somewhat grand hall is softened by the surrounding gardens of Howick, where perhaps the real passion of the place resides. They sweep around the hall on all sides, a pleasing as well as curious mix of shrubs and trees which are unfamiliar to the county. Successive generations of Greys were enthusiastic gardeners and each was responsible for adding hardwoods to the plantations around the hall, and interwoven with these plantations are woodland gardens carpeted with flowers. The effect of both tempers the imposing grandeur of Howick, particularly on its southern façade.

Howick was the home of the Grey family from 1319 until the death of the 5th Earl Grey in 1963. The house then passed to his daughter Lady Mary Howick. The house which bears his name dates from 1782, though its main section was completely gutted by fire in 1926. When it was rebuilt the interior was changed substantially but outwardly neither the house nor the gardens seem to bear any trace of scarring. The present owner, Lord Howick of Glendale, is as keen on trees as his forebears were but it was the 2nd Earl Grey, the Prime Minister responsible for the passing of the 1832 Reform Bill, who undertook the most ambitious tree planting at Howick. It was he who planted the long walk, a grand avenue of trees, which led eventually to the coast.

DUNSTANBURGH

The majestic ruins of Dunstanburgh Castle stand exposed to the sweeping winds that blow in off the North Sea along a shoreline rocky with gleaming whinstone. At one time Dunstanburgh boasted a harbour hewn out of the hard dolerite rock. Thomas, Earl of Lancaster, ordered the building of the massive castle in 1313. It stands on a promontory of basalt, one of the most easterly outcrops of the Great Whin Sill. The vast gatehouse of the castle was later, in 1380, converted by John of Gaunt into a keep. Fragments of this gatehouse survive shard-like, looming up to gaze out over the broad undulating links which stretch away to both north and south. The ragged profile of these ruins, with the more intact Lilburn tower on the north side, recall the buffeting sieges it suffered during the Wars of the Roses. In later centuries it fell into neglect, a romantic edifice which emphasized the brooding and solitary character of the surrounding coastline, captured in a watercolour by Turner. The castle ruins became a favourite nesting site for kittiwakes, guillemots and fulmar petrels.

A mile to the south, as if to break up the sometimes bleak aspect of Dunstanburgh, is the more homely fishing village of Craster, renowned for its smoked kippers. But these days few cobles go out in search of herrings for kippering; the fishing here is now the preserve of a very few.

CAPHEATON

Tomlinson describes Capheaton as a

truly Arcadian little village, consisting of a neat and comfortable row of model cottages, looking very picturesque with their carefully trained roses and creepers clambering up the walls beneath low, quaint overhanging eaves. The prospect from the village is exceedingly beautiful, extending over a portion of the park to the lake, with its woody islets and girdle of majestic trees.

This description is as apt today as it was when he penned these words over a century ago. The dovecote stands at the end of the village which dates from the late eighteenth century when it was rebuilt. The estate has been in the Swinburne family since the thirteenth century and it is known that Allen de Swinburne bought the original castle from Thomas de Fenwicke in 1274. In the struggle between Charles I and his Parliament, the Swinburnes took up the royal cause which led to the sequestration of the estate by Parliament in 1639. Sir John Swinburne, returning from exile after 1660, destroyed the castle to build Capheaton Hall. His architect, Robert Trollop, who also designed Netherwitton, used the old castle as his quarry. Lancelot 'Capability' Brown, who was born in nearby Kirkharle, was responsible for landscaping the grounds of Capheaton, one of a few such works he undertook in the county.

DUDDO

The Duddo Stones date from around 2000 BC and the five stones may have been asso-ciated with a burial site. Several Bronze Age relics have been discovered in the vicinity. Originally, there were thought to be more stones forming a circle some 10 metres in diameter. The stones are situated about 1½ kilometres from the tiny village. Stephen Oliver, writing in his *Rambles in Northumberland* in 1835, wrote

> On visiting several circles in the northern counties of England, I have noticed, that, though not erected on very elevated situations, they generally command an extensive prospect, and that a fire lighted within them would be seen at a great distance by the inhabitants of the surrounding country.

This is as true of the Duddo Stones as it is of the Warrior Stone at Ingoe and both seem to be popular with pipits, skylarks and wheatears. In the village, which is barely more than a farm and two or three houses, is a broken remnant of Duddo Tower and in the survey of 1541 it was recorded, perched on a rocky crag of some 100 metres in height, as belonging to the Claverings: 'At Duddo there standeth a pece of a tower that was rased and casten down by the King of the Scots.' The tower was destroyed in the war of 1496, and James IV would have noticed it on his way to Flodden, attacking the nearby castles of Ford and Etal on his way there. The tower was rebuilt around 1561 and much of it was still standing as late as 1888.

PITTLAND HILLS

On the hills above Wark on Tyne is the quiet village of Birtley whose church has a Saxon cross dating from around 700. In the vicinity are a number of earthworks, with names like Goodwife Hot or Male Knock Camp, which are among the earliest recorded place names in the county. Goodwife Hot may have been a description of the goddess of fertility, but many Celtic names were later corrupted either because they were not understood or because they were added to.

Also in the vicinity, on the fells above Birtley, is Pittland Hills which, as the name suggests, were once coal workings. At the same time as the land was being worked in this way, it was also being drained and more adaptable breeds of sheep were introduced to the uplands since they were to be the key element of the hill farming economy. A little lower down the slope from Pittland Hills is Birtley Shields, the suffix 'shiels' indicating the practice of summer pasturing. This activity was still widely practised well into the sixteenth century, even later in some places where farm improvements were slow in coming. With the introduction of buildings in stone on the uplands, settlement became permanent but it was still tough. According to Tony Hopkins, in his superb *Northumberland National Park* (1987) guide, the farm labourer had a single room and had no more than a small plot of land on which to grow vegetables to add to the diet. They were usually paid in kind, perhaps a sack of grain per month, and the hind, or worker, had to provide an additional member of his family as a worker, as and when needed. This more or less bonded labour system was to survive as late as this century in some places around here.

FALSTONE

The little village of Falstone sits beneath the Kielder Dam, within sight of its 52 metre high embankment which arcs through a width of over half a mile and keeps back anything up to 200 billion litres of water. The village is reached by a three-arched bridge, built across the North Tyne in 1844 to replace a ford. It was here that a fragment of a runic cross was found bearing the inscription, 'Eomaer set this up for his uncle, Hroethberht – Pray for his soul', written on one side in Roman unical letters, and on the other, in Anglo-Saxon runes. It has been suggested that the cross was erected at a time when Pagan runes were fast disappearing before the influence of Latin Christianity brought by St Augustine and his followers. The stone cross was discovered in 1812 by the local Presbyterian minister, possibly on the site of an old chapel. After 1814, Falstone became a separate parish and a new church and rectory were built. Attendants included dogs as well as people. In *Waters of Tyne* (1991) T.H. Rowland describes how the shepherds would bring in their dogs who remained quiet until the final blessing when all rose and pandemonium broke out. After a while it was decided that everyone should remain seated for the blessing. In the graveyard here are a number of finely sculpted headstones, one of which is known as the 'dance of death', the work of a talented but unknown mason.

NOTES ON THE PHOTOGRAPHY

The majority of these photographs were taken between New Year and May 1992 using FP4 and HP5 film stock. The camera used was a 35mm Leica M4P with a 35mm lens. The exposures were mostly determined by ambient light readings on a Minolta III flash meter. There are a few pictures which date from an earlier period and these are reprinted here by kind permission of Robert Lewis & Co. of Hexham. These are Carrshield; the River Allen at Cupola bridge; Ingoe; Mohope; Langley Castle; and Langley on Tyne. The prints were made by Roberto Marcotullio of Studio Roberto in London.

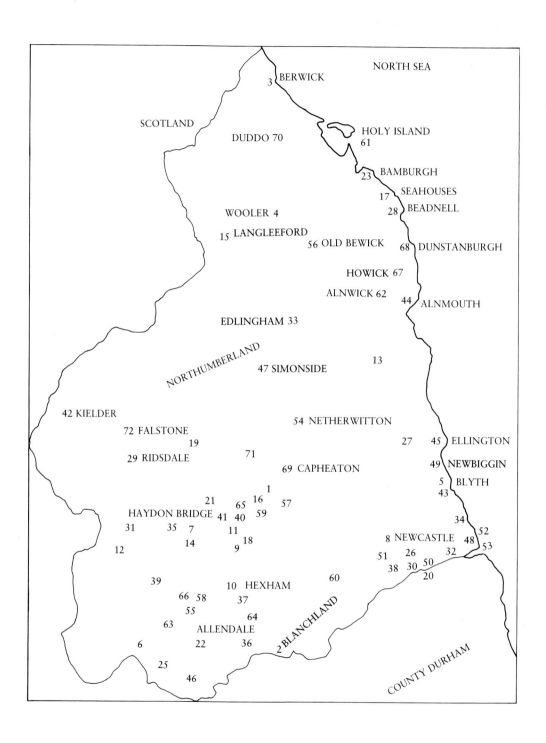

NORTH SEA

3 BERWICK

SCOTLAND

DUDDO 70

HOLY ISLAND
61

23 BAMBURGH

17 SEAHOUSES

28 BEADNELL

WOOLER 4

15 LANGLEEFORD

56 OLD BEWICK

68 DUNSTANBURGH

HOWICK 67

ALNWICK 62

44 ALNMOUTH

EDLINGHAM 33

NORTHUMBERLAND

47 SIMONSIDE

13

42 KIELDER

54 NETHERWITTON

72 FALSTONE

19

29 RIDSDALE

71

27   45 ELLINGTON

49 NEWBIGGIN

5 BLYTH
43

69 CAPHEATON

1

21   65 16   57

HAYDON BRIDGE 41 40 59

34

31   35   7   11

52

12

14   9 18

8 NEWCASTLE 48

51   26   32   53

38   30 50

39

60

20

10 HEXHAM

66 58   37

55

64

63

ALLENDALE

BLANCHLAND

6   22   36   2

25

46

COUNTY DURHAM

TECHNICAL DATA

PAGE NO.	MAP NO.	TITLE	CAMERA	LENS	SPEED	F STOP	FILTER
III	1	SWINBURNE	LEICA M4P	35mm	1/60	5.6	
VI	2	BLANCHLAND	"	"	1/125	16	
1	3	BERWICK-UPON-TWEED	"	"	1/250	16	
3	4	WOOLER	"	"	1/125	8	
5	5	BLYTH	"	"	1/60	11	
7	6	NINEBANKS	"	"	1/125	16	
9	7	LANGLEY CASTLE	NIKON F3T	24mm	1/250	16	RED
11	8	JESMOND	LEICA M4P	35mm	1/250	11	
13	9	CHOLLERFORD	"	"	1/60	11	
15	10	HEXHAM	"	"	1/4	2	
17	11	RIVER NORTH TYNE	"	"	1/125	8	
19	12	COANWOOD	"	"	1/15	4	
21	13	COLLIERSDEAN	"	"	1/250	16	
23	14	LANGLEY ON TYNE	"	"	1/125	815	
25	15	LANGLEEFORD	"	"	1/60	5.6	
27	16	SWINBURNE ESTATE	"	"	1/60	11	
29	17	SEAHOUSES	"	"	1/60	8	
31	18	CHOLLERTON	"	"	1/125	11	
33	19	HARESHAW BURN	"	"	1/30	8	
35	20	WALLSEND	"	"	1/125	11	
37	21	STEEL RIGG	"	"	1/60	11	
39	22	ALLENDALE	"	"	1/30	2	
41	23	BAMBURGH	"	"	1/60	5.6	
43	24	BYKER	"	"	1/60	11	
45	25	MOHOPE HEAD	"	"	1/250	16	ORANGE
47	26	NEWCASTLE	"	"	1/60	5.6	
49	27	ASHINGTON	"	"	1/125	11	
51	28	BEADNELL	"	"	1/60	8	
53	29	RIDSDALE	"	"	1/60	16	
55	30	NEWCASTLE	"	"	1/250	1	
57	31	ALLENBANKS	"	"	1/30	4	
59	32	NORTH SHIELDS	"	"	1/125	16	
61	33	EDLINGHAM	"	"	1/125	16	
63	34	CULLERCOATS	"	"	1/250	16	
65	35	HAYDON BRIDGE	"	"	1/30	11	
67	36	HEXHAMSHIRE COMMON	"	"	1/250	16	
69	37	HEXHAM	"	"	1/60	11	
71	38	NEWCASTLE	"	"	1/15	4	
73	39	RIDLEY COMMON	"	"	1/30	4	
75	40	CHIPCHASE ESTATE	"	"	1/125	5.6	
77	41	BLACKCARTS	"	"	1/250	16	
79	42	KIELDER	"	"	1/125	16	
81	43	BLYTH	"	"	1/30	11	
83	44	ALNMOUTH	"	"	1/30	8	
85	45	ELLINGTON	"	"	1/60	11	
87	46	COALCLEUGH	"	"	1/30	16	
89	47	SIMONSIDE	"	"	1/125	16	
91	48	NORTH SHIELDS	"	"	1/60	8	

PAGE NO.	MAP NO.	TITLE	CAMERA	LENS	SPEED	F STOP	FILTER
93	49	NEWBIGGIN-BY-THE-SEA	"	"	1/125	16	
95	50	THE QUAYSIDE, NEWCASTLE	"	"	1/60	8	
97	51	NEWCASTLE	"	"	1/125	11	
99	52	NORTH SHIELDS	"	"	1/125	16	
101	53	THE FISH QUAY, NORTH SHIELDS	"	"	1/250	16	
103	54	NETHERWITTON	"	"	1/60	11	
105	55	BRIZLEE HILL	"	"	1/250	16	
107	56	OLD BEWICK	"	"	1/250	16	
109	57	INGOE	NIKON F3T	24mm	1/250	16	RED
111	58	HIGH STAWARD	LEICA M4P	35mm	1/15	4	
113	59	GUNNERTON	"	"	1/8	5.6	
115	60	BYWELL	"	"	1/125	16	
117	61	HOLY ISLAND	"	"	1/15	4	
119	62	ALNWICK	"	"	1/125	16	
121	63	MONK WOOD	"	"	1/60	16	
123	64	WHITELY CHAPEL	"	"	1/30	8	
125	65	CHIPCHASE	"	"	1/30	11	
127	66	RIVER ALLEN	"	"	1/30	16	ORANGE
129	67	HOWICK HALL	"	"	1/60	8	
131	68	DUNSTANBURGH	"	"	1/30	16	
133	69	CAPHEATON	"	"	1/30	8	
135	70	DUDDO	"	"	1/60	16	
137	71	PITTLAND HILLS	"	"	1/60	16	
139	72	FALSTONE	"	"	1/60	16